D1526806

PERGAMON INTERNATIONAL LIBRARY
of Science, Technology, Engineering and Social Studies
The 1000-volume original paperback library in aid of education,
industrial training and the enjoyment of leisure
Publisher: Robert Maxwell, M.C.

Modest Technologies
for a Complicated World

THE PERGAMON TEXTBOOK
INSPECTION COPY SERVICE

An inspection copy of any book published in the Pergamon International Library will
gladly be sent to academic staff without obligation for their consideration for course
adoption or recommendation. Copies may be retained for a period of 60 days from
receipt and returned if not suitable. When a particular title is adopted or recommended
for adoption for class use and the recommendation results in a sale of 12 or more copies,
the inspection copy may be retained with our compliments. The Publishers will be
pleased to receive suggestions for revised editions and new titles to be published in this
important International Library.

Other Titles of Interest

A Pergamon Journal of Related Interest

WORLD DEVELOPMENT

The Multi-Disciplinary International Journal devoted to the Study and Promotion of World Development

Chairman of the Editorial Board:

Dr. Paul Streeten, The World Bank, Washington, DC, USA

Scope: *World Development* encourages the publication of original articles and review papers which help to stimulate and improve development and appropriate science and technology in developing countries. Development must be redefined as an attack on the chief evils which afflict mankind today: malnutrition, disease, illiteracy, slums, unemployment and inequality. And it must not neglect non-material values, like cultural traditions and national identity. It is the purpose of this journal to analyze those forces which hinder or promote development and international integration. Contributions develop constructive ideas for experiments and innovations in social and cultural institutions, standards, and styles of life and work.

Modest Technologies
for a Complicated World

by

ROBERTO VACCA

PERGAMON PRESS
OXFORD · NEW YORK · TORONTO · SYDNEY · PARIS · FRANKFURT

U.K.	Pergamon Press Ltd., Headington Hill Hall, Oxford OX3 0BW, England
U.S.A.	Pergamon Press Inc., Maxwell House, Fairview Park, Elmsford, New York 10523, U.S.A.
CANADA	Pergamon of Canada Ltd., Suite 104, 150 Consumers Road, Willowdale, Ontario M2J 1P9, Canada
AUSTRALIA	Pergamon Press (Aust.) Pty. Ltd., P.O. Box 544, Potts Point, N.S.W. 2011, Australia
FRANCE	Pergamon Press SARL, 24 rue des Ecoles, 75240 Paris, Cedex 05, France
FEDERAL REPUBLIC OF GERMANY	Pergamon Press GmbH, 6242 Kronberg-Taunus, Pferdstrasse 1, Federal Republic of Germany

First published Ed. Rizzoli, Milan 1978 (Italian)

First English Language Edition 1980

British Library Cataloguing in Publication Data
Vacca, Roberto
Modest technologies for a complicated world. —
(Pergamon international library).
1. Underdeveloped areas — Technology — Social aspects
I. Title
301.24'3'091724   T14.5   79—42741

ISBN 0—08—024067—4 (Hardcover)

Set in 11 on 12pt Baskerville by
Express Litho Service (Oxford)
and printed and bound in Great Britain by
William Clowes (Beccles) Limited, Beccles and London

Contents

Introduction

FEW businessmen or statesmen would enter a gambling casino, select just any game and start playing without giving any thought to the rules of the game and how fair or unfair they might be.

The economic games of society are played according to rules which are often arbitrary and unfair, which have been agreed upon after a struggle among different groups and therefore mirror ancient compromises or which have even been chosen almost at random. And yet statesmen, businessmen, the public at large — all of us are taking part in these games without many qualms. We only object to the rules when we think they are harming us: in many cases, though, we have no reliable information based on which we can decide whether this impression we have is right or wrong.

We may hope that statesmen do not patronize gambling casinos, but we see them taking decisions, which appear rational only if we accept the doubtful rationality of the rules of the economic game.

I will try to point out in the following chapters possible new rules of national and international economic games.

For about two centuries technology has played a major role in our societies. Its progress has staved off the limitations imposed by diminishing returns. Now we see many signs of trouble. Modern technology, as it has evolved, appears incapable of preventing the occurrence of serious crises: unemployment, unmanageability of systems which become too large or too complex, pollution, exhaustion of resources. A solution may be found, perhaps, in reductions of size: in making technology more modest.

Modest — also called intermediate or alternative — technologies have been proposed in recent years for application both in industrialized and in less developed countries. In the latter, the main goal is to create a large number of jobs, achieving a very low investment per employee (typically a few hundred dollars, rather than many thousands of dollars). In industrialized countries the proposed aims are: full employment; a reduction in the size of production units — in order to improve working conditions; a reduction of waste; a reduction of the energy and non renewable resources content of products; the introduction of standards for grading products and services according to their usefulness or their harmfulness, so that the more harmful ones can be eliminated or modified. This latter assessment is very difficult to implement, as it entails the long term evaluation of any possible external diseconomy affecting not only contemporary third parties, but also future generations. We cannot ignore that the problems posed by the exhaustion of natural hydrocarbons within a few decades (unless present trends are radically changed) are just a portion of the global problem to be solved, which again includes technological problems as just another portion.

Proposals for modest technologies have obvious ethical motivations in less developed countries. The aim is to give something to populations which have nothing, in the sense that their *per capita* income is $300 or less. Jan Tinbergen has observed that the average yearly *per capita* income of the richest 10% of world population is 13 times higher than the average yearly income of the poorest 10%. Apart from considerations of distributive justice, it appears unlikely that unbalances of this proportion may be preserved for a long time in the contemporary world, with its fast and abundant communications so that relative deprivation is rapidly and deeply felt by the poor.

The basic question to be solved is the survival of the planet and a prerequisite to the solution is the attainment of equilibrium in the socio-political situation and also in the demographic, energy, agricultural, soil preservation, exploitation of resources and recycling processes.

I strongly disagree with those who admit the possibility of boundless growth in one or more fields of human activity — even if they do not reach the extremes of H. Kahn, who considers as plausible in less than a century a world population of 20 billion people, with an average *per capita* income of $20,000 per year, that is: almost three times the present day average for the United States.

Meanwhile economists and decision makers see only the critical problems of today — particularly the inflation-unemployment dilemma — and they are insensitive to long term problems.

One of the central long term problems is whether mixed economic systems are really unstable in conditions of full employment and whether there are no alternatives to the existence of structural unemployment at such a level as to contribute heavily to global unemployment, when inflation rates are relatively modest. In recent years we have seen that our faith in the stability of the Phillips curve (which expresses the inverse proportionality relationship between percent unemployment and percent annual price rise) was too optimistic. Phillips diagrams, which were acceptable in the Sixties, were not even plotted for annual price rises of more than 10%. These, however, have been surpassed in the Seventies and have been accompanied by unemployment levels of 6 to 8%.

This situation is less tragic than the one prevalent after the great depression of 1929 in many Western countries (where unemployment reached 15% and even 20%, depending on the year and on the industrial sector considered). However, it represents a symptom of the failure of fiscal and monetary regulatory mechanisms, due to which neo-classical economists had affirmed that "everywhere in the free world governments and central banks have shown they can win the battle of the slump" and that "just as we no longer meekly accept disease, we no longer need accept mass unemployment" (P. Samuelson, *Economics,* 6th edition, Chapter 17, p. 337).

G. Mensch has suggested recently that the transition from boom to recession and then to depression may be caused by lack of innovation during the expansion phase. In a boom, industries attempt to exploit as much as possible the economies of scale and, consequently, to expand their markets (confining innovation to superficial improvements of products) until such a time when markets are bitterly fought for, profits fall, investments are blocked and liquidity frozen. Only as a last resort at the very pit of depression will industry turn again to massive applicative innovation, tapping the large reservoir of unused basic inventions constantly produced by scientists in each industrial sector at the rate of a couple per decade. There is no doubt that in the last two centuries the major economic booms have coincided with the opening of new industrial fields (steam engines and heavy mechanical industry; electrical industry; chemical industry; electronics).

It might be argued, then, that a gradual and continuous introduction of innovation in industry could serve the purpose of doing away with economic depressions and of keeping unemployment levels below acceptable thresholds (1–2%) without causing very steep annual price rises. On the other hand this solution is very hard to steer in a mixed economy, without transforming it *ipso facto* into a centrally planned economy, and it concerns only marginally the less developed countries. The massive introduction of industry in third and fourth world countries would represent, indeed, a very significant innovation, which is desirable, but can be implemented only over the long term.

One of the reasons why maximalistic solutions of this type cannot be rapidly implemented — apart from the resistance of old timers and the problems of training and education — is that the necessary capitals are not available for investment. Consequently modest technologies, featuring a low investment per employee, could help solve deeply felt problems both in advanced countries and in less developed countries.

Historically the attempt to transfer basic scientific inventions continuously to technological innovations has not been made explicitly. Modest technologies, though, did exist and they represented the entire industrial universe, say, until the beginning of the first industrial revolution. We may well ask, then, why modest technologies have been replaced completely by modern hard technologies, instead of surviving and continuing to offer the advantages, at present indicated as desirable by their advocates. The first factor here is that modest technologies are unfit for the production of advanced and sophisticated equipment and also for the production of heavy machinery. Secondly, the higher productivity typical of modern technologies rewarded most manufacturers who abandoned traditional methods of production. Thirdly, renewing modest technologies or preserving them in a society characterized by large numbers (of population, of area, of density, of products demanded by the market) is a large organizational problem and, until the present time, adequate motivation for solving it has been lacking.

The present time appears particularly well suited to a reintroduction of modest technologies for two reasons. The first is that advanced industry (heavy, hard, high volume) can produce quickly good and inexpensive tools to be used in modest technology manufacturing ventures. The second reason is that the serious organization problems above referred to, can now be solved with the help of modern systems engineering and organization procedures which have been developed only in comparatively recent times.

Any individual problem of introduction or reintroduction of modest technologies will have to be examined critically. Feasibility, productivity, costs, standardization, specifications, quality control and transportation needs will have to be assessed. It cannot be affirmed that any modest technology, introduced anywhere and in whichever context is appropriate and desirable.

Modest technologies are often claimed to avoid alienation of the industrial worker. Nobody has really proved, though, that the quality of life enjoyed by people who work for small outfits using modest technologies is better than that of employees of large organizations employing advanced technologies.

We should do more than just consider job environment and economic conditions for citizens of advanced nations, and food availability for citizens of the fourth world. This is a reductionist error. We should also evaluate education and instruction levels in that they determine the average human quality of any population, which is a prerequisite to an acceptable way of life. The average cultural level of a population also influences its employment situation: the higher the culture — the lower hard-core unemployment and technical obsolescence of workers.

In this vein, cost/benefit analyses should not consider only goods and services which can be easily evaluated in monetary terms. Criticisms of the very concept of gross national product are well known. Paul Samuelson wrote (*Economics,* 6th Edition, p. 793): "The best measure of growth is real GNP, qualified by data on leisure, population size, relative distribution, quality and non economic factors."

Recently many proposals have been made in order to define concepts of gross national wellbeing, incorporating the factors indicated by Samuelson as well as: mobility, instruction levels, efficiency and level of service of public utilities and services, availability of cultural opportunities and of green spaces, absence of pollution, scarcity of crime, etc. Of course the evaluation of non economic factors is difficult as it depends on subjective assessments, so that it may entail the collection of data on indifference curves actually prevalent in a given population. This task could be carried out by means of polling and of demoscopic analysis. We know well that these procedures are not very reliable, but this should not be a deterrent. On the contrary it is urgent that new pragmatic definitions of gross national wellbeing be introduced and employed as soon as possible, even if at a later stage we will have to recognize the need to revise them.

We should also include in the GNP factors that are easy to quantify but are normally overlooked (e.g. maintenance and improvements to buildings carried out by private parties for their own use), and exclude waste, at least as represented by actual destruction of goods. A more general definition of waste would again have to be based on subjective judgement.

We should also remember that the attribution of costs and prices to goods and services is to a large extent illusory —

and so is the reliance on them to the end of steering market mechanisms through the regulatory function of supply and demand. In fact both in mixed economies and in centrally planned economies price structures are largely arbitrary, with some prices set very low for social or demagogic purposes and others strongly increased through taxation. It cannot certainly be claimed that the resulting process is optimized with respect to any imaginable criterion and particularly in order to obtain a reasonable and balanced use of resources. J. K. Galbraith in *The New Industrial State* has maintained that inefficiencies in the use of resources, caused — among other things — by the implicit price fixing activities of large technostructures, are a minor disadvantage. The resulting high levels of profit offer, instead, marked advantages in that they make possible a recourse to advanced technologies and the high investments that, in turn, exert a positive influence on productivity. No one has yet proved, however, that the trends observed by Galbraith can guarantee an acceptably reasonable planning over an acceptably long term so that society as a whole can reach a coherent set of goals.

We should not accept as a dogma that modest technologies are advantageous: rather we should prove the point by means of examples of successful applications. Apart from gathering and recording such examples, we must classify the sectors in which the use of modest technologies appears more advantageous, and also plan and design new applications after having carried out cost/benefit analyses, taking into account the possible effects of interventions in the price and cost structures of the region or country we are considering.

The elements to be assessed for judging new intermediate technology initiatives, are:

— return on capital, which should be high as invested capital is supposed to be low
— productivity, particularly considering the effect on this factor of possible incentives, which could mask the real situation

- effect on employment and employability
- adverse factors, like higher costs for organization, inventories, quality control, transportation, etc. Note here that marketing organization and expenses will represent a critical issue: on one hand they are an integral part of production cost, on the other hand they can vanish if intermediate technology producers are guaranteed given volumes of sales — which would represent a very massive incentive.

Modest technologies stand a good chance of being introduced in: agriculture and processing of agricultural products; public works and road construction, small buildings, chemical and manufacturing industry; recycling of waste and raw materials. Modest technologies can also be applied in energy production (solar water heaters, windmills, small total energy modules).

By using modest technology we will be able to gain considerable advantages. At the same time we will have to run many risks: of having unwittingly chosen solutions which are quite far from optimum ones (and of having wasted scarce capitals) and of having introduced in the market unreliable objects or equipment. We will not be able to do without advanced technology nor without modest technologies: the problem is to define the right mix of the two. Paradoxically the success or failure of industrial enterprises (modest or advanced) depends on the accounting procedures that are employed, more than on the ability of the people who work in them. There are no simple rules for innovating in reasonable and advantageous ways. We must carry out critical analyses: of technology, administration, applied science and organization. We must know traditional disciplines as well as modern procedures for coping with complexity in all its forms.

In order to make our complex society more rational, simpler and more modest, we need to go through very complicated pieces of reasoning.

CHAPTER 1

Modest Technology

THE American engineer was rich and full of creativity. He had settled in Sarkhan — a small country between Burma and Thailand — and he had realized that the most critical problem to be solved, if the Sarkhanese economy was to be improved, was that of bringing water to the good plots of land on the hills. Instead of importing American pumps, he made an agreement with a Sarkhanese mechanic and they began to manufacture pumps made with pistons taken from the engines of old jeeps, with bamboo pipes and driven from an ordinary bicycle through a simple gearbox. The bicycle could be quickly disconnected from the pump and used again for locomotion. This was very important because the Sarkhanese are poor and cannot afford more than one bicycle per family. From this modest beginning, the Sarkhanese economy began to take off and the relationships between Sarkhan and the United States became a lot better than they would have been otherwise.

Homer Atkins, the American engineer, had been also to Vietnam about ten years after World War Two. In Vietnam too he had seen what was needed. There was need of small factories for the production of bricks and of modest stone quarries. The Vietnamese also needed many small food canning plants, so that the agricultural produce from the Northern countryside could reach Saigon. There was need for short narrow roads that would permit the inhabitants of the coast, where the soil is acid and unsuitable for cultivation, to reach the very fertile land in the interior. There was no need for large dams nor for wide military roads.

1

Homer Atkins was right — but nobody ever paid any attention to him, also because of the fact that he never existed. He is, in fact, one of the characters in the book *The Ugly American* written by Bill Lederer and Eugene Burdick in 1958.

The Ugly American was an important book in which the authors explained to Americans, in simple terms and with fictional examples, what they should have done and what they should have avoided in Southeast Asia. If Lederer and Burdick had been listened to, if their pragmatic analysis of the errors made by the French in Indochina had been taken seriously, perhaps there would have been no Vietnam war. I do not cite the Lederer and Burdick book to rewrite history hypothetically, but because in the story of the ugly American the concept of intermediate — or modest — technology was stated in a clear and convincing manner. Lederer and Burdick were forerunners of the economists, planners, essayists, organization experts and manufacturers, who in recent years contributed professional studies, projects and concrete examples of the simple solutions of practical problems.

This was not the first time that novelists introduced innovative ideas which were later taken up concretely by engineers or by statesmen. In such cases we usually say that these ideas were in the air and that anyone could have voiced them or written about them. It may be true. Perhaps it is also true that innovative ideas should be sought for everywhere — even in novels — and judged on their merits rather than on the identity of the originators.

The irrigation problem solved in the imaginary country of Sarkhan can be considered a textbook case. To use a wasted resource, like the engines of jeeps abandoned after a war, and to use better — that is for a double purpose: in time sharing — a widely available resource like the bicycle, was certainly the right thing to do. The aim was to increase agricultural production and the resources used — material and labor — were all local: there could be no doubt that the scheme made sense. If the Sarkhanese case was not fictional, it could well serve as a paradigm for any application of modest technology. The investments were insignificant and the entire management of the project was in the hands of the local population, which gained self confidence through this experience and — we can imagine further — began to get familiar with simple mechanical problems from which it could proceed to more complicated tasks and get training also useful in other fields.

Introducing modest technologies in a country where none exists is certainly a good thing, particularly if the investment needed is almost zero. The Sarkhanese case, however, is a limit case. In practice we will find that investments, even if modest, are greater than zero and therefore we have the problem of choosing the direction in which to aim them. In general we will find also more or less advanced pre-existing technologies. We shall, therefore, weigh whether and to what extent it is better to try and strengthen the existing technologies or to replace them with new modest technologies. Naturally there is also the question of which new and modest technology should be introduced first and in which field.

Every decision on the eventual introduction of modest technology in a given economy will also be influenced by the pre-existing employment situation. If unemployment — or underemployment — is very high, you cannot go wrong: almost any new proposal of this kind will be accepted and priority should be given to those projects which promise to produce faster results. So you will have to evaluate in advance the effect of each new type of modest technology on the employment level, as well as its acceptability by workers and public powers. It will also be appropriate to forecast the effects on productivity, *per capita* gross product, level of instruction, etc. If unemployment is not the number one problem in the society we are considering, we must decide to which segment of the labor force we had better try and introduce modest technology.

Here we have the difficulty that often employment statistics are not reliable. Not all those listed as workers actually work. Not all those registered as unemployed abstain from any activity or get their only income from the dole. In the absence of reliable data, the very proposal for the introduction of a new modest technology can serve as a useful criterion, since the number of people who accept it represents an index of their previous levels of income and activity.

Probably each type of modest technology can find wide enough application where previous levels of unemployment, productivity, income *per capita* are above or below certain thresholds, the existence and the values of which have to be determined experimentally.

The problems of unemployment, of productivity and of raising sufficient capital for investment exist not only in backward economies and in less developed countries, but also in the developed and industrialized nations. In advanced nations innovative choices are more difficult to implement, because there are already complex production and marketing organizations which are heavily conditioned by their earlier history. If we try to replace these organizations with others, we come in conflict with established interests — real or imaginary — and certainly with the inertia of the system and of the people who make it work and with every kind of tradition and habit.

Possibly considerations of this kind can be considered as belonging to the domain of tactics, and therefore of scarce importance and of temporary interest. However, there are certainly strategical plans to be defined concerning: the type of organization necessary for the introduction of modest technology in an economically advanced society and the costs of this organization; the productivity and the competitiveness of modest technologies with respect to traditional ones; the *per capita* income obtainable by workers who use modest technology and the possible effect of the introduction of modest technology on a large scale, on average national income levels; and, finally, the distribution and the marketing of products manufactured with modest technology, the organization for controlling their quality, and the ways in which the introduction will affect the mechanisms of supply and demand.

The concept of modest technology, then, has been in the air for some twenty years. It would appear that the introduction of modest technology in some countries could only do good.

In advanced countries it would seem that the introduction of modest technology, or the return to it, might offer advantages as well, but only if certain conditions are satisfied and certain precautions observed.

The purpose of this book is to discuss, and when possible to determine, what are the conditions which must be satisfied and what precautions must be taken, so that the introduction of new modest technologies in the third world — as well as in the first or the second — can be implemented on the basis of concrete and pragmatic evaluations. The decision of implementing modest technological innovations should never be taken on vague ideological grounds, just because the general idea sounds good and modern or satisfies certain abstract, perhaps only aesthetic, criteria.

CHAPTER 2

In Our Heads We Have More Than Just Our Mouths

IN ancient times men worked alone or together with animals to produce energy with their muscles: to plough the land, to transport objects, to raise buildings, to excavate and mine, to produce artifacts. Man applied to each of these activities not only his physical energy, but also his intelligence and his information in order to steer the flow of energy towards the desired aim. Even in the primitive civilizations of ancient times it was often uneconomical to use a man in order to produce just energy: this was done and it is still done marginally, as in the case of a man who turns the handle of a winch for lifting some heavy object.

At present men produce raw or brute energy with their own muscles almost exclusively during emergencies or for very simple and accurate jobs or for pleasure — as in sport. We can derive, however, a numerical evaluation of the economics of energy generated by man, based on the present value of raw energy produced by electrical power stations.

A strong man working for many hours a day can produce at most a power of 100 watts. If we suppose that he works for 10 hours a day, he will then be able to produce 1 kWh of energy per day of work.

At current prices, 1 kWh of energy is sold for less than 10 U.S. cents: this sum, then, represents the daily wages a man would earn by producing raw energy, for example cranking around the shaft of a dynamo in order to charge batteries. The yearly salary of a man who makes 10 cents a day and works a 6 day week, is $30.

In the poorest countries of the world — like Ruanda and Upper Volta — the average gross product *per capita* per year is about $60. A Ruandan worker will earn about $300 per year or 10 times more than he would if he were employed to produce just raw energy. It is meaningless, then, to try and evaluate a man simply on the basis of the amount of energy he can produce with his own muscles.

Today we fear grievous famines in the less developed countries of the world and we know that world reserves of wheat are critically inadequate, even though crops were very good both in Russia and in America in 1976 and in 1977. More and more often we read classifications of humans based on the amount of food they can dispose of during one year. We know that the average need for wheat is 300 kg per year for each inhabitant of the globe. However, in the poorer countries many humans find it hard to secure 200 kg of wheat per year — which is a bare minimum. In the United States the average consumption per inhabitant is 1,000 kg of cereals per year, of which 200 kg are consumed directly and 800 kg indirectly, in the sense that they are used as fodder for poultry and for cattle.

This unbalance in the availability of food is certainly staggering and certainly we should do something to guarantee enough food to every person in the world. If this problem is not solved, we cannot hope to solve any other problem. Populations which are malnourished or continuously threatened by famine cannot be improved in any other way. We cannot expect their productivity to increase. We cannot hope that their social consciousness be awakened, nor that they participate significantly in any decision.

We cannot believe, however, that the problem of food is the only one to be solved: it is the first one — but there are others. If we consider men simply as digestive tracts, we commit a serious sin of minimalism. It is devoid of sense to think of man simply as a mouth to feed, or simply as a producer of useful work, or as a number to be entered in a statistical table. Other human abilities can produce results and performance which go a long way beyond mere survival. A single man — of course adequately nourished — but also educated and exposed to the impact of culture and inventiveness, can produce constructive ideas capable of making available the bushels of wheat necessary to hundreds of thousands of his fellow men.

Once we have recognized this truth, we cannot continue to speak of the quality of life just in terms of material standards of living. We must also speak of the quality of human life in that its improvement can produce better intellectual performance and also participation in decision processes. Men can participate in each endeavor and in each activity only with what they have and what they know. It is essential that people know more, so that they can participate more. In one with the elimination of economic and social injustice, it is necessary that large masses of people should reach higher levels of education and instruction. Only after that, they can understand the world, evaluate and check the actions of technocrats and decision makers — and also form a true public opinion on all the problems and the crises looming over contemporary associated life.

To reach this aim we need a massive program of generalized instruction, some orders of magnitude more ambitious than all the programs ever attempted or dreamed of before, which will allow all men to live not only in a society capable of survival — but also in a just and open society.

Unfortunately we hardly see any sign of a program of this kind being started anywhere in the world.

Even if a similar program were to be started, we should seriously doubt whether it would have any hope of success — not so much because of its novelty and size, as because of the opposition that seems to be evoked by the very idea of generalized learning. We have, then, to consider more realistic and shorter term solutions to the most pressing problems around us.

The majority of vital requirements of less developed countries are abundantly available in advanced countries: food, artifacts, medicines, machine tools, technical know how. Only food and artifacts can be transferred from one country to another without difficulty — apart from the problem of paying for the goods supplied. International economic aid consists largely of food and artifacts. The transfer of technical know how and the export of machine tools or production facilities all imply a transfer of culture and a deeper level of cooperation.

Advanced countries — apart from needing innovation, that will reinstate certain modest technologies or that will apply scientific inventions — also need many natural resources which are to be found in less developed countries.

Less developed countries — apart from needing food, medicines and manufactured objects — need technology transfers from advanced countries in order to be able to take off economically.

On the other hand, whenever a less developed country takes off economically, it not only makes advantages available to its own inhabitants: it also offers benefits to advanced countries, because it begins to represent a new market.

Before we look into the special initiatives necessary for the introduction of modest technologies in advanced and in non advanced countries, I shall try to evaluate the impact of international economic aid and the probability that a new international economic order may be established.

CHAPTER 3

International Aid and a Possible New International Economic Order

"INTERNATIONAL economic aid programs are the means by which the poor of rich countries send money to the rich of poor countries."

This wisecrack is a few years old. It is cynical, but it mirrors at least some traits of reality. Equality of opportunity certainly has not been achieved completely in advanced countries: it cannot even be seen dimly on the horizon of many less developed countries.

Wisecracks are no use for solving the many problems we meet in the field of international economic aid: on the other hand the views of many respected experts are plausible — and contradict each other. In 1956, the U.S. Senate gave a grant to the Center for International Studies of the Massachusetts Institute of Technology to carry out a study on foreign aid. One of the most important results of the study was to be the definition of a criterion for deciding whether to increase or not the aid sent to a given country. The Center suggested that economic aid is to be granted and if necessary increased, provided two conditions are present. The first condition was that the country's government should have taken adequate measures for raking an important portion of any income increase in order to route it towards new investment. The second condition was for that government to have prepared a general development plan.

Milton Friedman noted (in his article "Foreign Economic Aid: Means and Objectives", in *The Yale Review*, Summer 1958) that the United States throughout their history would never have fulfilled these two conditions. Consequently the

10

United States would have never qualified for receiving economic aid from other countries. Friedman implies that actually the United States have never received any economic aid from abroad and he contends that any other country — poor and backward though it is — could duplicate the American success and achieve, on its own, development and progress.

I do not think that things are so simple. Actually the craftsmen, the farmers, the technicians, the doctors, the other professionals — who emigrated to America by the million particularly during the last century — brought with them the investment in their professional training made in their native countries. This was a massive economic aid that the United States received mainly from England and from Central Europe. Without it, American history would have been very different from the one we know.

One of the best known international aid programs was the Marshall Plan for the reconstruction of Europe, to which the United States contributed with 11 billion dollars from 1948 to 1951. The Marshall Plan was so well known probably due to its good success — although in its conclusive phase the aid it gave was mainly of a military character. From 1945 to 1972 the United States have given aid to other countries for a total amount of 146 billion dollars — which corresponds to a little less than 1% of the global gross national product for those 28 years.

The concept that international aid had to be increased and that it had to be directed towards productive applications and not towards military ones, spread more and more in United Nations circles after World War Two. In 1959, the UN declared that the decade 1960—69 would be the development decade and invited the richer nations to contribute 1% of their gross national product as aid to less developed countries.

In 1964, the economist Raùl Prebisch, who was then Secretary General of UNCTAD (United Nations Conference on Trade and Development), had determined that the annual rate of development of less developed countries could have reached 7% (instead of the 5% foreseen by the UN plan for the development decade), if industrial nations increased their aid to the level of 1.5% of the gross national product. In this hypothesis, less developed countries could have reached in about forty years the same *per capita* income Europeans had in 1964. Prebisch also proposed a stark reduction of military expenses on the part of all industrialized nations — including socialist countries.

It is well known that all this never happened. Aid to third world countries stayed much below 1% of the gross product of advanced countries. The gap between European and third world average incomes has become much larger. The story of these failures, as well as many interesting expert opinions on the subject, can be found in a reader collected by John A. Pincus: *Reshaping the World Economy* (Prentice-Hall, 1968).

The Sixth and Seventh Special Sessions of the UN have approved resolutions to the effect that the establishment of a new international economic order is desirable and necessary and concerning an action program to attain it. Although these resolutions were approved with no contrary votes, it appears that present chances of enforcing the application of the new Charter of Economic Rights and Duties of States are rather remote. In view of the existence of conflicts of interest between nations and also of excessive inequalities in standards of living and access to resources, the Club of Rome has sponsored a large study conducted under the leadership of Jan Tinbergen (Nobel Prize laureate for Economics in 1969) and financed by the Dutch government, on the Reshaping of the International Order (RIO).

The ratio between the average *per capita* income of the richest 10% and the 10% poorest of the world's population is at present 13:1. If this ratio is not drastically reduced during the coming decades, not only will it be impossible to guarantee economic stability in most countries, but also political stability will be in jeopardy. We are witnessing, in fact, a revolution of rising expectations featuring well known symptoms of relative deprivation, which are reinforced as a consequence of easier and faster communications and, therefore, easier comparisons between life styles and standards.

One of the results of the study by the Tinbergen group is that even levying from advanced countries a voluntary tax of the order of 1% of their gross national product and transferring it to developing countries, the ratio quoted above of 13:1 would take 40 years in order to be reduced to a value of 3:1. This updates the Prebisch evaluation of 1964 and indicates how steeply the situation has worsened in the last fifteen years. Four decades represent, in fact, ample time for any unstable situation to deteriorate and lead to disruptive phenomena (see on this subject: Jan Tinbergen – "Assigning World Priorities: Theory and Application", in *Annals of the New York Academy of Sciences,* Vol. 261, 1975).

The RIO Report consists of four parts which describe:

– the need for a new international order and its causes
– the possible ways in which to achieve the necessary changes
– the proposals for action on issues that have the highest priority, like poverty and inflation
– the ten major areas that are relevant to the establishment of a new international order and for which the appropriate decisional level is not regional or national, but can only be found on an international level.

The Tinbergen group suggests that in some cases it will be necessary to establish new supranational organisms and authorities. Since, however, many of these organizations already exist, but only work on paper, it will also be necessary to form new coalitions – not only among nations having related interests, as in the case of OPEC – but also among groups that have never cooperated in the past. These new cooperation efforts could represent a decisive factor for the concrete implementation of the prescriptions dictated by the supranational authorities.

An example may be given by a cooperation between Western agricultural organizations and FAO for accelerating the build up of reserves of food stocks as suggested by the World Food Conference held in Rome in 1974. Another example could be a cooperation between consumers' unions and international organizations like UNCTAD and GATT for reducing impediments to importing products from developing to developed countries.

The goal of the Tinbergen group was to produce a document less generic and less maximalistic than those produced by third world countries. The RIO Report is based on sound and authoritative scientific grounding, so that it may be accepted both by industrialized and by developing nations and it may constitute a neutral basis for discussion and an occasion for further exchanges of ideas between third world and industrial nations.

The RIO Project tries to single out interventions and innovations which will:

— eliminate bottlenecks
— produce a multiplication effect, unleashing further action in allied areas and/or regions
— produce concrete results within a short term.

The aims of RIO are pragmatic and any suggestion arrived at through a process of scientific analysis will be translated as far as possible in politically significant and feasible terms — without necessarily having to reach a quantitative expression for the results achieved. The RIO Report contains no formal model of any of the areas or processes dealt with. This may appear curious in view of Tinbergen's econometric background. Jeremy Bray, the British MP, has made the comment (in his paper "The Logic of Scientific Method in Economics") that Tinbergen has veered off from the Keynesian approach of producing scientific theories by induction from particular observations and generalizations and has introduced in the field of economics the logic of deduction-falsification, a more rigorous corroboration of models by the evidence and a goal seeking feature of analysis.

The RIO approach is far from neutral with respect to values. Probably it could not have even tried to attain value neutrality, without losing all significance.

One of the most important final goals set by the RIO Project is equality of opportunity for different countries, in the same way as at present it is assured to some extent to the citizens of certain countries. In the passage from the national to the international level, difficulties grow considerably, as we miss labor movements and democratic participation in decision making. These two factors, however imperfectly, tend to achieve at the national level a certain equality of opportunity. At the international level we also lack taxation and a central bank.

On the other hand it is well known that at the present time, even within individual countries, social and political structures need to be analyzed and redesigned, as is evidenced by at least two trends. The first trend is towards a demonstration democracy (as suggested by Amitai Etzioni) and, beyond that, towards an increased level of direct action and eventually of militant political violence motivated by relative deprivation (as suggested by Ted R. Gurr). The second trend is towards the establishment of alternative power structures, not through revolutionary actions, but through a quasi natural process of duplication, so that traditional structures (parliamentary, of regional government) go on existing, while their traditional functions are now carried out following different sets of rules in a precedent setting context by other structures (direct negotiations between workers' unions and governments, action of citizen groups united in consumer or conservation movements, etc.). These new national informal structures may foster the establishment of innovative international structures, only in that they also set the precedent of successful innovation.

It may be argued, though, that what is needed at the international level is — on the contrary — a shift towards a higher formalization of the structures and a firmer attribution of power to them. Enforcement of decisions taken by old and new international bodies should be done legally, instead of giving to these organizations purely advisory charters, as for example in the case of the advisory code of the International Chamber of Commerce, which is not noted for being followed too scrupulously.

While we argue the necessity of establishing new international authorities, we may note with some hope the so called explosion of a negotiation mood at all levels: political (to settle armed conflict), commercial (to settle problems of tariffs, etc.) and in the field of labor relationships (at least in certain countries). I. William Zartman in *The 50% Solution* (Anchor Press-Doubleday, 1976) has collected an interesting series of essays on national and international negotiations and also on negotiations with terrorist groups.

State nations may be induced to relinquish part of their sovereignty and accept that it be attributed to international bodies, because of internal pressure from groups of opinion makers (possibly including political parties) or because of external actions. These, in turn, may be represented by the use of force — or the threat of using force — or by the force of reasoning exerted in open discussions in the international arena, tending to reach multilateral agreements based on long term compromise.

It would be advantageous to all concerned if it could be proven to industrialized nations that creating a new and more equitable international order is in their own self interest. This, however, can only be claimed to be true over the longer term. Over a short term, devoting 1% of an advanced nation's gross national product to aid less developed countries (or even 2% as has been proposed by the Argentinian Bariloche Foundation) will cause the income of its citizens to decrease.

Even if no country resorts to the resources blackmail (natural resources from the third world, agricultural products from North America, high technology products from North America, Europe and Japan) a further downgrading of the food-population situation may well take place in the near future. Then famines could kill tens or hundreds of millions of people in Southern Asia and Africa. This would have a massive impact on world public opinion and would force more energetic aid actions to be taken in the future, possibly as a consequence of campaigns on the part of pressure groups internal to advanced countries.

In a positive vein we can stress that developing countries

represent an interesting future market for advanced countries. The RIO Project contains some explicit, measurable and convincing statements to this effect. An important underlying assumption is that the process of renewing or reshaping the world order may be started and implemented without losing faith in international institutions — shaky as they may be. This assumption should not be taken as an indication that the RIO Project is utterly utopian: in fact RIO contends reasonably that reshaping the world order now is a much better proposition than getting into World War Three and postponing the renovation effort to the following post war period.

The ten areas of concrete action which are considered as having first priority and which are discussed in the fourth part of the RIO Project are:

- international monetary system
- income redistribution and financing of development
- industrialization, trade and international division of labor
- food production and distribution
- energy, ores and minerals
- defense of the environment
- ocean management and protection
- transnational enterprises
- scientific research and technology transfer
- arms reduction.

The authors of RIO suggest that five new international authorities be established:

(1) A *central world bank* which would create reserves available to various countries following procedures similar to those used for Special Drawing Rights and which would supervise the use of these reserves for achieving goals collectively defined and agreed upon, like financing third world development.

At present the functions of world central bank are carried out to a large extent by the United States. Many less developed countries will be occasionally considered not worthy of credit based on subjective considerations. For example, Chile received no financing from the World Bank during the Allende administration. It received from Western countries financial assistance of only 109 million dollars in 1973 (increased after the coup to more than $1 billion per year). It received from the Inter-American Development Bank, $11 million in 1971, non financing in 1972 and 1973, and again $97 million in 1974.

(2) *A central world treasury* having the right to levy taxes and to use taxation proceeds as a means to equalize opportunities for nations. Without a central world treasury, it is highly unlikely that any country — and in particular countries with centrally planned economies — would increase their aids to third world countries.

(3) *An international industrial development bank,* which could carry out a meaningful action only if it was possible to: achieve a higher mobility of labor and of capitals; negotiate simultaneous multilateral agreements concerning the prices of basic products, beginning with oil and wheat and covering eventually all the 18 basic products which have been singled out by UNCTAD. The international development bank should also promote a greater local processing of local resources in order to increase the average portion of the final price (at present about 10%) which third world countries actually receive.

(4) *A world food authority,* which would have decisional and prescriptive powers (not at present vested in FAO) and could order the production and conservation of adequate reserves of cereals, coordinate the definition and the adoption of population planning policies, and contribute concretely to the achievement of an agricultural growth rate of 3% a year in third world countries.

(5) *A world energy research authority* intended to coordinate research on alternate energy sources carried out in different countries, avoiding duplication of efforts, contributing to overcome national legislation difficulties (like those that in the United States have stymied prospection for new geothermal energy sources) and participating in negotiations on the prices of all types of energy.

Transnational enterprises carry a considerable weight in

the world's economy. They handle, for example, 27% of all the world's exports (47% of primary products and 20% of manufactured goods exports). At present the operation of transnational corporations poses problems, which to be solved require innovations in legislation as well as in attitudes and habits, so that reasonable compromises can be reached.

It is well known that transnational enterprises have contributed considerably to transfer modern technologies to developing countries. Their impact in this field had been probably more important than that of governments. On the other hand it is well known that transnational enterprises often get advantage from the disparity of legislation in different countries and, particularly, from the lack of modern laws (like antitrust laws) in certain countries. The general interest of populations — particularly of developing countries — would be served by reasonable guidelines imposed to the further contributions, which transnational enterprises will certainly be able to give to development.

When we speak about development of backward countries, we should not look only at economic development or at the increase of *per capita* gross national product — as I anticipated in the last chapter. It is important that the transfer of modern technologies and the upgrading of cultural levels of third world countries be not confined to the lower and simpler fringes of technology and of science. They should also cover the more advanced fields of activity and of research. First class research institutes should be established in the third world, possibly concentrating their research on third world problems.

Derek J. de Solla Price (in his book *Little Science, Big Science,* Columbia University Press, 1963) supplied an interesting proof of the fact that scientific development will not continue to grow over the long term, at the same rates which we have experienced during the last century. Scientific development can be measured in terms of: number of active scientists, number of technological and scientific publications and papers appearing every year, investment levels in research and development. In fact the efforts invested by the more advanced countries in scientific research, have been doubling every ten to fifteen years — whereas it is well known that the population doubles every 150 to 200 years in those countries. Paradoxically — were this trend to continue indefinitely — in a few decades all the population of advanced countries would be active in scientific research, with no one left to take care of agriculture, industry and services. De Solla Price concludes, then, reasonably that there are only two directions in which we can hope to proceed, if science is to go on developing over the long term. The first is fostering scientific development and research in the third world — as already said. The second direction is towards scientific contributions supplied by women, who at present are very few in scientific and technical fields.

After this brief presentation, you may feel that the RIO Project is a quite maximalistic endeavor or proposal. Perhaps only maximalistic efforts will be adequate to provide antidotes against the socio-economic instability of the planet and against future conflicts.

The first two reports to the Club of Rome (Forrester and Meadows' "Limits to Growth"; Mesarovic and Pestel's regionalized hierarchical multi-level world model) had tried to evoke positive reactions on the issues of external limits to development and of interdependence of policies, interventions and actions on the international scene. These reports reached a wide public opinion, but failed to evoke enlightened actions by governments. It appears reasonable now to try and stir more active interest through a discursive commonsensical approach — based, however, on the best available information and conceptual economic, social, technological, legal and scientific opinion.

The work carried out by the Tinbergen group seems to indicate that the very concept of the nation-state is outdated and is not compatible with peace and prosperity, in a world whose parts are more and more interdependent. We have already examined some mechanisms through which nation-states might renounce a portion of their sovereignty. This, however, cannot be the only component of a global solution.

I have tried to show that we cannot avoid attacking simultaneously a large number of critical problems, whose complexity is such that we cannot hope to define deterministic procedures capable of bringing us to optimum solutions. Any innovative study of the general condition of the world, and in particular of the conditions of developing countries, will have to possess some characters of a prescriptive manifesto. Then the well known difficulty of forecasting the future in an increasingly complex world, appears to be even greater — when we try to predict the future success of a manifesto which is rational, pragmatic and — duly — complex. The RIO Report, in fact, does not try to get acceptance and popularity on the basis of easy slogans or of a play on passions, which would be hard to control.

Naturally, the difficulty of the task and the complexity of the problems are not the only obstacles to the implementation of a new and more just international order. Countries with higher *per capita* incomes tend to protect their positions and do not share the enthusiasm for a more equitable distribution of resources, nor for an increase of the international aid some of them are already giving to less developed countries. These resistances on the part of rich countries may be said to be prompted simply by self interest, but they are rationalized by means of processes which Karl Marx would have called ideological and which Vilfredo Pareto would have classed as derivations. We cannot rid ourselves of the arguments against the establishment of a new international order, simply by stating that they are ideological or that they are dérivations. We shall have to take a closer look.

Apart from Milton Friedman[1], one of the more vocal opposers

[1] Curiously Milton Friedman was awarded the Nobel Prize for economics in October 1976, while the RIO Project was presented in Algiers during a meeting of the Club of Rome. A group of third world economists wrote and handed around during the Algiers meeting a document in which they deplored the decision of the Nobel Prize Committee accusing Friedman of having worked as a consultant for the tyrannic government of Pinochet and of being unworthy of that high international kudos.

of the concept of a new international economic order is Robert W. Tucker, professor of international relations at Johns Hopkins University. Tucker published a book in 1977 called *The Inequality of Nations* (published by Basic Books) in which he presents the following arguments:

— historically, interdependence has favored conflict rather than avoid it and it has never opened the way to peace and order
— order has always been based on military and political power
— recently Western countries refrain from using the power they certainly would have. They do so obeying to a current egalitarian fashion and yielding to the pressure of intellectual groups within their own population
— these pressure groups are motivated by a confusion between political and opportunity equality which has become a reality in the last two centuries in most Western countries (while it is unknown in most of the third world) and equality among nations. Third world countries are only interested in equality among nations.

Consequently we can anticipate only two mutually exclusive alternatives. The first is that conflict situations, caused by interdependence, will maintain the whole world in a chronic state of chaos. The second alternative is that a world power will play the role of custodian of the world's order. Tucker suggests that the Soviet Union could well try to take that role. He proposes that Western countries should oppose any such Soviet attempt and should realize that they have already granted to the third world considerable economic and social benefits. According to Tucker, the expansionist policies of Western countries have not been imperialistic nor purely motivated by the desire to exploit underdeveloped countries. Tucker suggests that Western countries should not even discuss possible reparation payments to third world countries. They should rather play again their historical role of regulators and custodians of order.

Tucker's viewpoints are at least as debatable as those presented by Tinbergen and other proponents of a new international order.

It is true that the transfers of technology, of culture and of life styles from Western to third world countries have been advantageous to the latter to some extent. On the other hand these advantages have been mixed blessings. Not only culture, technology, tools, machines, medicines and finished products have been exported to the third world. Essentially the West has exported proliferating complexity, but has not been able to export the means for managing complexity – because it lacked them and, to some extent, it still lacks them. The last chapter of this book discusses decisional problems for complex socio-economic-technological systems and the modern procedures which can be applied in this field.

I would like to conclude that attempts to blueprint a reshaping of the international order have certainly to be made, even if we cannot guarantee their success, nor evaluate their chance of success. From this we have to derive another consequence: that we should not limit ourselves to large scale attempts of this kind. Neither can we affirm – as Tucker does simplistically – that only two different scenarios can be imagined for the world's socio-economic future. We do not have many certainties and so we must look simultaneously for many different types of answers. One of the partial answers is the definition, the design and the cost/benefit assessment of modest technology enterprises – which is one of the subjects treated in the balance of this book.

CHAPTER 4

Small May Be Beautiful–Does It Always Make Sense?

"ARE you so sorry because you are so short?" — is the first line of a sonnet by Giuseppe Gioacchino Belli, the great Roman vernacular poet. The sonnet goes on to say that being short is an asset, because you need less material for your clothes and because you can manage to enter theaters unnoticed without paying your ticket.

E. F. Schumacher (a former economic consultant to the British Coal Board) has suggested, in his 1973 book, that *Small is Beautiful.* His thesis is that giant nations and giant corporations are not as good for people as smaller countries or smaller production and marketing outfits, which need low investments and use simpler technologies. The sub-title of Schumacher's book is: *A Study of Economics as if People Mattered.*

Schumacher's name is the first to be mentioned whenever the subject is modest technology — and rightly so. He was the first to say a number of things that made a lot of sense and he had complemented his Oxford schooling in economics with concrete involvement in management, in organization, in industry. *Small Is Beautiful* is, then, an important book. Unfortunately, though, it contains many lightheaded statements, it presents many points of view that are wrong and it tries to carry out a number of doubtful analyses. I think the book has so many faults that, because of them, many readers could be induced not to take seriously or to discard many of the serious and correct arguments introduced by Schumacher. In the present chapter I will try to single out some problems which

Schumacher just has failed to see and I will indicate which of his viewpoints are sounder and which of his intuitions were more fortunate. I will conclude the chapter listing the errors which I think Schumacher has made and which, however, do not necessarily invalidate the soundness of his basic argument. The basic argument would suffer indeed, if all those erroneous lines of reasoning were considered as an integral part of it: this is the reason why I thought it was appropriate to give this warning.

It is curious that with all his fixation on small units and all his opposition to bigness in every field, Schumacher did not devote even a few lines in the whole book to overpopulation and to the need for birth control policies. He notes reasonably that a further accelerated development of advanced countries creates worse problems than the development of backward countries. He does not mention, though, that a large portion of the increases in consumption of natural resources and of energy is just due to the population increase.

Schumacher never mentions either systems engineering or systems science. He seems to be almost unaware of the existence of large technological systems. He notes naively that any third class engineer or research worker is able to cause complexity to grow, but you need a certain flair and a true intuition in order to simplify things again. Now, if we are speaking of the large technological, organizational and economic systems which exist today, flair and intuition are certainly necessary, but they are by no means sufficient for simplifying them. We need advanced and sophisticated techniques like those used in systems engineering.

Schumacher has not seen these questions and it is useless to try and find them in his book — as it is useless to look in it for neutral and strictly balanced judgements. This becomes obvious when we notice that a big deal is made out of the civil and economic success of small nations, independent from larger neighboring nations which were about to engulf them, but didn't (see the cases of Belgium and France; of Denmark and Austria with respect to Germany) — whereas no mention is made of the civil and economic failures of other countries, which are just as small.

But let us proceed to the many right things Schumacher has said and to the proposals he has made and waved around passionately like flags. After all, if his *modus operandi* had not been paradoxical, he would not have been guilty of the omissions I have indicated, but he would not have singled out the very important points which form the core of his book. Perhaps he would not have worked — as he did for years — for the practical application of his viewpoints and his intuitions with his Intermediate Technology Development Group. This is a private non profit organization, active in studying and promoting alternative modest technologies which can be employed particularly in third world countries.

It was Schumacher who introduced the expression "intermediate technology", which he defined as production made by the masses — as a substitute to mass production — and more explicitly as a technology capable of:

— creating jobs in places where people already are and not in overpopulated cities
— requiring a low enough unit investment per workplace, so that a high number of jobs can be created. This is particularly important in countries which have massive and endemic unemployment: the main goal is then to maximize employment levels and not to maximize productivity
— being implemented with fairly simple production methods so that it is not necessary for workers to go through long and expensive training periods, which may also be next to impossible because of a lack of instructors
— using raw materials locally available for producing goods which are actually in demand on the local market.

Schumacher stresses very much that it is not right to make large investments, which create a small number of jobs with a very high unit productivity, in countries where unemployment is the basic problem. He contends reasonably that the investment necessary for the creation of one new job should be of the same order of magnitude as the yearly income earned by the worker who fills that job. There is no deep motivation for this. It is simply reasonable that every year, one tenth of the salary of each worker be put aside and accumulated in view of creating another job over a 10 year period. If, instead, the creation of a new job requires a capital ten times larger than his yearly income, accumulating one tenth of that salary every year would lead to the creation of another job only after 100 years — which would be too long.

At present the average investment required to create a new job in advanced countries is £2,000. Third world countries should plan to invest on the average 10 times less, or £200.

In support of this view, Schumacher quotes the case of India, which has a gross national product of about £16.7 billion per year with a population in excess of 600 million. In a 10 year period the population of India increases by more than 100 million people. Then it would be necessary to create at least 50 million new jobs every 10 years — or 5 million new jobs a year. It is difficult that investments intended to create employment may exceed 5% of the gross national product, as Schumacher reasonably points out. In 10 years, then, these investments should add up to one half the present level of gross national product — or £8.35 billion. The investment for the creation of each job should be, then, about £170 — that is somewhat less than one tenth of the average investment required to create a job in advanced countries.

All these points of view are quite reasonable and the quick computations concerning availability of capital and investment needs, presented by Schumacher, are very good first approximations — even though other consequences of the population explosion in India are not made explicit and highlighted, as they deserved to be.

Then Schumacher criticizes most preventive cost/benefit assessments and says that they are wrong because in them:

- non renewable resources (like oil and other minerals) are
  considered as current income, rather than as a capital
  belonging to the whole of mankind
- costs are often underestimated, in that they do not include
  present and future external diseconomies
- the equivalents of renewable or non renewable resources,
  products, services and even intangibles like human life and
  artistic treasures are expressed as money values.

These arguments are reasonable too, although often cost/
benefit assessments — which are affected by much deeper and
basic faults as I will try to prove in Chapter 9 — are exempt
from the defects Schumacher finds in them. In fact, in order
to introduce essential intangibles — like human lives — in quantitative computations, there is no need to attribute a very high,
or infinite, value to them. This would only introduce excessive
complication — and no real meaning — in the formulas. It is
feasible, instead, to impose the conservation or the achievement of conditions concerning intangibles as a constraint to
the objective function that we are trying to reach.

Schumacher proposes, instead, the much weaker alternative
of introducing in the assessment purely qualitative considerations and of accepting them at least with the same weight which
we attribute to quantitative factors. The obvious objection is
that qualitative considerations are much vaguer and more
elastic than quantitative measurements or evaluations and,
then, they can be so debatable that it is easier to base on them
long controversies, rather than fast decisions generally agreed
upon.

Another argument against the so called modern hard technology used in industrialized countries is that it damages the
human environment and tends to stifle human nature, which
eventually reacts, revolting against technology. Schumacher
quotes a statement by Pope Pius XI, according to which, matter
comes out of industrial plants improved, whereas people come
out of the plants debased and corrupted. This point of view
too is debatable. I think it depends on what type of plants

one has been in or on what type of tales one has heard concerning industrial plants. I have worked in many industrial plants where I have learnt a lot and I have taught a lot, improving myself and helping to improve others. It could be argued here that I am speaking only of intellectual improvement, and not of moral or spiritual improvements. I can counterobject that it is just in industrial plants that many workers have acquired general culture, political training and awareness of their rights. Then they may have used this training and this awareness in ways which may not all have been reasonable, but which certainly do not lead to fighting blindly against the plant or against industry in general.

Intermediate or modest technologies have to be chosen intelligently. We all agree on this score and we shall go on agreeing up to the point at which we try to proceed from this generality to concrete indications of which choices are intelligent and which choices are stupid. Schumacher gives a few examples of intelligent choices. The most convincing example is the one of a large earth moving job (for building roads or a dam) in a country in which unemployment is massive and chronic.

The first solution would be to employ a few hundred specialized workers, to invest many million dollars in bulldozers, trucks and other earth moving equipment and to complete the job in one year's calendar time. The second solution consists in investing only a few hundred thousand dollars in modest tools (picks, shovels, barrows, small conveyor belts, pneumatic drills with a built in gasoline engine so they do not require a large compressor) and in having many tens of thousands of workers use them. The second solution could require roughly the same calendar time as the first to complete the job and would have the additional advantages that the initial investment is lower and that the creation of very many new jobs — also for manufacturing and maintaining the modest tools — would produce consistent multiplicative effects. The argument makes sense because it gives a first approximation numerical evaluation. Rereading Schumacher's original and my rendering of it, I realize though that I have put the relevant numbers in the example — he had not.

Schumacher gives some more examples: small oil refineries processing from 5,000 to 30,000 barrels per day; small plants for producing up to 60 tons of ammonia per day. As we shall see, there are many other examples which are even more interesting.

Schumacher is right when he says that intermediate technology cannot find universal application. It cannot be applied to the typical products of modern sophisticated and advanced industry. He is wrong, though, when he affirms that the products of this type of industry normally do not satisfy any essential need of poor populations. In fact the products of the more advanced pharmaceutical industry may well be essential for the very survival of a population; a communication network (telephone, telegraph, radio) may be very important for the economic take-off of a country, but could certainly not be built and installed with modest technologies.

Another quick calculation, jotted down on the back of an envelope — as Schumacher says — concerns the effectiveness of foreign aid in bringing actual benefits to developing nations and the share of the corresponding investment ideally received by every citizen of a country that receives the aid. If we subtract from the total of foreign aid every contribution that does not really go to the economy — like, for example, military aid and armaments — Schumacher estimates that, dividing the total aid given by Western countries to third world countries by the number of inhabitants of the latter, one gets a unit contribution of about £2. Even if we multiply this amount by 2 or by 3 (and we have seen in Chapter 3 that the question is complex and hotly debated), the effectiveness of this aid in producing an economic take-off or in improving significantly the present extreme poverty, would be quite marginal. It would be much more effective, instead, to reroute a certain percent of aid from its present forms (food, manufactured goods, machines) to new forms. These would consist of gifts of knowledge, not transmitted in writing but by groups of people defined by the combination: A, B, C. A is for Administrators, B is for Business-

men and C is for Communicators, that is: teachers, populari-
zers, professionals in charge of training programs. Schumacher
figures that even earmarking only 1% of international aid for
organizing and running the gifts of knowledge program, a few
million pounds would accrue. This would be enough to obtain
considerable results — certainly better than present ones, which
— paradoxically — are achieved almost exclusively by the
generous initiative of private groups.

Schumacher gives other reasonable suggestions and mementos:

— of establishing in each developing country not just one
  new type of industry or one new enterprise, but many
  different ones simultaneously, so that multiplicative
  effects can be produced and at least some new industries
  will be each other's customers;
— to spread the message that quality of life is not just proportional to the number or the value of objects, of buildings, of durable goods and of services we have at our
  disposal. Consequently we should not turn down proposals
  for change in the organization, in the structure and in the
  rules of society — just because they appear to imply a
  decrease in the average standard of living. We should try,
  rather, to assess the probable long term effects of these
  changes on the stability of society and on the quality of
  spiritual life.

This proposal of Schumacher is a bomb — of course. Taken
together with the following one, it represents a proposal for the
establishment of a new tradition and of new habits. It represents
a program for a mental hygiene treatment for the masses and
for individuals. I have tried to broadcast a similar message in
a book called *Handbook For An Improbable Salvation* without
significant results.

— to recognize that industrial, economic and cultural development represents only the tip of an iceberg, which would
  not emerge at all, were it not for its enormous underwater
  bulk. In this simile the submerged nine tenths of the iceberg

represent education, organization, habits, fashions and standardized relationships which involve or affect the entire population of a country.

This last point is very important and very relevant. I am instead, in total disagreement concerning the ways proposed by Schumacher for raising cultural levels. I think it is important to make this point clearly, because the basic common sense, the honesty and the learning of Schumacher cannot compensate for the superficiality and the downright mistaken approach taken in these proposals.

The raising of cultural levels, according to Schumacher, should be centered only on humanistic culture, on spiritual values and on general ideas of structures and relationships by means of which we should all think.

Obviously Schumacher had very vague ideas concerning science and technology. Sometimes he mixes them up one with the other or he identifies either with procedures for producing know-how — that is with operational procedures enabling anyone who follows them to do something — not necessarily to know something or to understand exactly what he is doing and why.

It is not so by a long shot. I think it is necessary to tell it like it is in order to avoid confusion as well as loss of time in inconclusive discussions with people who have heard that mathematics and physics are pseudo-sciences, but do not really know what they are all about. It would be very nice if we could reach a clear understanding of mathematics, physics and natural sciences without the trouble of being trained in these sciences — but unfortunately it is not possible. The vague and general ideas that one manages to grasp while remaining at the border and possibly reading popularizations written by professional scientists — which are not always very well done — cannot be really used as a basis for constructive thinking. Schumacher was convinced of the contrary of the statements I have just made and he tried to confine in the class of parlor games, not only scientific experiments and their interpretations, but also physical theories, the research procedures of physicists and chemists and even the epistemological consequences of all this learning. He even went so far as to say that the knowledge of the second law of thermodynamics cannot add anything to a man's mind and does not contribute at all to the internal development of man. This statement is a very damning one, because it proves that its originator does not know what he is talking about (and does not know that there is no second law of thermodynamics, but a second principle of thermodynamics, and the two things are very different); because a man who can think complex thoughts is better developed internally than a man who cannot; finally, because the knowledge of thermodynamics enables us to take better decisions concerning energy problems. A more efficient energy management can improve dramatically – and perhaps even save – the life of many human beings. And yet Schumacher thinks that Shakespeare's poems are so full of vital ideas that we miss our life if we ignore them. These poems are presented as much more important then thermodynamics. I certainly do not despise Shakespeare's poems – but I do not think they can help us at all to solve large and critical socio-economic problems.

Schumacher says that the great ideas which have allowed man to understand the world, society and life itself, are:

- the idea of evolution from lower to higher forms, which can be applied systematically to all aspects of reality without exception
  the idea of natural selection and of the survival of the fittest
- the Marxist idea that all the higher manifestations of human life have an economic origin and motivation
- the Freudian interpretation of all the higher manifestations of human life as dark stirrings of a subconscious mind
- the general idea of relativism, denying all absolutes
- "the triumphant idea of positivism, that valid knowledge can be attained only through the methods of the natural sciences and hence that no knowledge is genuine unless

it is based on generally observable facts. Positivism, in other words, is solely interested in 'know-how' and denies the possibility of objective knowledge about meaning and purpose of any kind."

I have had to transcribe word for word the last point, because I would have been unable to digest a statement which is so twisted and unfocused. The five previous points, which I have condensed, also appear to be generic and are, in fact, barely recognizable as a rendering of the ideas of Darwin, Marx, Freud, Einstein — of which, presumably, they are supposed to represent the gist. It is curious that Schumacher, like others who insist that we need to understand nature (and they are right), rejects the very tools with which we have managed to understand at least some aspects of reality: physics, chemistry, mathematics.

I agree that a good scientific training is no automatic guarantee of ethical behavior, of goodness, of altruism. On the other hand these are not the goals of scientific training. Not many people reach the higher levels of goodness, of altruism and of ethical behavior and those who do are not necessarily very learned. However, if a correlation exists, probably the more cultured people (particularly if they are scientifically cultured) should be able to behave more responsibly — and ethically — at least because in a complex world they are better able to foresee the consequences of their actions.

To instill in people principles of humane behavior, of goodness, of altruism, nothing better has been found — apart from example — than edifying talks or speeches. This is, then, a discursive or literary approach — certainly not a scientific one. This does not mean, though, that these discursive-literary presentations could carry out the functions of science and technology. At most we can say that the reverse is true: those who have a good scientific or technical background could be quicker in grasping edifying talks.

Schumacher talks also of Buddhist economics and, again, I find him very difficult to follow. The Buddhist doctrine, according to Schumacher, states that work in general should have the following goals: the development of the higher human qualities and faculties, the pursuit of goals in common with other people and, finally, to produce goods and services. Now: the development of higher human faculties, the establishment of good human relationships, liberation (from taboos, from myths), artistic creativity, are all worthwhile goals. They are rather difficult to achieve even following the traditional paths of imitating good examples and of meditating on the thoughts of the best among us. It is very naive to hope that these improbable goals can be reached by means of industrial work — even if it is technologically innovative.

Schumacher has another proposal which is even more naive. He would like to see productivity go down by a factor of 6, because less productive work would not be so hectic and stressing: it could be carried out with calm, with enjoyment, with creativity — even making things beautiful. We would produce, however, as much as at present — if the number of hours worked was also multiplied by 6. Here the little hasty computation carried out by Schumacher just does not work out.

His argument is as follows. At present in an advanced country only 3.5% of the total time available to the population is used for productive work. In fact: only half of the total population is employed — actually works. Of that half, only one third works for producing goods, as the other two thirds only provide services or are employed on things other than real production. And, finally, actual working hours are only one fifth of the total time of a worker. So:

$$\frac{1}{2} \cdot \frac{1}{3} \cdot \frac{1}{5} = \frac{1}{30} \text{ or } 3.33\%$$

If we work out what it would mean to increase 6 times the number of hours worked, this is what comes out. We should reach, of course, a total time of hours worked which is 20% of the total available time. Suppose, then, that we have not just half the population working, but 4/5 or 80%. (This means anyone who is fit would have to work: men, women, old people and children.) Let us suppose that 3/4 of the work force (instead of 1/3) is employed in actual production — which would mean that we would have to renounce a lot of catering, information services, a lot of performers or entertainers, and so on. Even then all these people — including children and older people — would have to work a six day week at more than 9 hours per day. I would consider this as a big step backwards, that the public would just reject — unless we decide to call "productive work" also any artistic activity or any way of getting fun. But this would just mean juggling names — not innovative thinking. Things appear in a very different light, when one makes explicit all the relevant numbers — and computes them right.

All the same, the positive part of Schumacher's thought is important, just as the practical work carried out by his Intermediate Technology Group. I think that often Schumacher and his followers are striving towards goals which are quite reasonable — but do so for the wrong reasons. It is not a grievous fault. Those who strive to reach harmful goals — whatever their motivations — are guilty of a much worse fault.

Let's not frown too much, then, when we find in the conclusions of *Small is Beautiful* an apologetic passage to the effect that the way to salvation goes through the four cardinal virtues: prudence, justice, fortitude and temperance. The first to talk about these virtues was Plato, who inspired St. Ambrose and then Thomas Aquinas and the whole official Christian thinking for many centuries. All these people had specialized in proposing edifying qualitative speeches — but they have not scored major operational successes in all these centuries. Even when apparently the majority of Western populations followed Christian teachings, the four cardinal virtues did not inspire the actions of too many people. At present I think that the Christian tradition is losing ground, so that it is unlikely that enough people — having disregarded the exhortations of preachers and spiritual leaders — will suddenly begin to follow similar exhortations when they are made by a British economist.

I think it is more reasonable to quantify all our arguments with the right numbers and to use all the available rational tools to understand reality and possibly to modify it to the common advantage. It is very risky to be behind the times and to make decisions on the basis of ineffective criteria, which could be tolerated in a world considerably simpler than the present one — whereas now they would lead to downright immoral actions.

CHAPTER 5

The Debatable Neutrality of Science and Technology

MORTIMER Taube suggested in 1961 — in his book *Computers and Common Sense* (published by McGraw-Hill in 1963) — that it would be appropriate to remove any restriction to the use of the term "science" to define any field of human interest or activity. Anyone should be able to call himself a scientist, if he so wishes. At present, instead, these words have a magic character and if one manages to be recognized as a scientist, then he finds it easier to avoid being branded as a crank — even if he is actually a crank. Taube concluded:

"If being a scientist were no more remarkable than being tall or short, fat or thin, the word 'science' could not be used to peddle nostrums to a gullible public. An activity carried out by any public or private body would then be evaluated as an activity, and its sponsors could not hide from scrutiny or frighten off investigators by insisting on the pure scientific nature of their intentions."

Unfortunately, nobody listened to Taube and consequently there are still many controversies on the opportunity of calling "science" some field of research or other.

There are also discussions to decide whether technology — as it exists in industrialized countries after its well known evolutions — is neutral, or is conditioned by the ideology which prevails in those countries, or, perhaps, is itself the factor which determines or creates those ideologies. This latter process — according to some — is designed to bring advantages to privileged classes or groups.

Some contend that the neutrality of technology is a myth,

shared also by decision makers and planners in countries with centrally planned economies in Eastern Europe. According to them, this is the reason why the industrial development in communist countries has followed so closely the Western industrial models.

I think that the question of the neutrality of science and technology cannot be debated along general lines. It cannot be debated by means of global allusions to certain historical events or situations. This question must be debated pragmatically, analyzing any eventual individual mechanism of interdependence between theories, beliefs and social principles on one side and technologies, productive and organizational structures on the other.

I think we should analyze critically many points of view which are currently accepted without discussion. They concern both the present technological and industrial situation and many proposals or plans for future alternatives.

Many people accept as a proven fact that modern industry and current technologies unavoidably produce massive external diseconomies. These are economic burdens (damages or liabilities, interrupted production of previous income, new expense necessary for preserving the *status quo*) and non economic burdens (risks having unknown probabilities, non quantifiable inconveniences and snags) which industrial companies cause to third parties or to the community in general (environmental downgrading). Now: external diseconomies are certainly produced by many human activities and, in particular, by many industrial and productive activities. We must not forget, though, that external diseconomies and environmental damages are not a constant and proportional feature of any industrial activity. Some of them produce less diseconomies than others. If we conceive and enforce appropriate laws and rules, we are often able to eliminate completely certain diseconomies. This has been proved in recent years in many countries and notably in England with the application of the Clean Air Act.

On the other hand there is no inherent guarantee that with modest decentralized technologies we will automatically elimi-

nate or decrease external diseconomies. To move in this direction we should make explicit all the consequences of the new
technological processes and check that their introduction would
improve the global socio-economic situation. This is a very
difficult task, as almost any activity we can think of will produce advantages in one field and disadvantages, possibly of an
entirely different nature and magnitude, in other fields.

One of the basic points to be discussed here is the ultimate
goal — or the set of the ultimate goals — of economic activity.
It is easy to criticize traditional economists and industrialists
because they behave as if social development and economic
growth were exactly the same thing. The two concepts do not
coincide, but we cannot have an adequate socio-cultural development if economic development stays below a certain threshold.
We should be careful, then, not to fight economic development
too harshly, because we would run the risk of preventing also
many desirable socio-cultural developments. In fact the success
of business ventures in general is far from guaranteed from the
beginning (when it is guaranteed beforehand, the entrepreneur
is normally a monopolist — or a crook). We should not be surprised, then, if the persons responsible for a business whose
success is not guaranteed by devious means, try to exploit any
possible rationalization, any device to increase efficiency or
any innovation which can give some hope of an advantage.

I think we should interpret in this sense the famous exhorta-
tion of Lord Keynes in his 1930 essay *Economic Possibilities
for Our Grandchildren* (republished in: Keynes, J. M. — *Essays
in Persuasion,* The Norton Library, 1963, p. 372):

"For at least another hundred years we must pretend to
ourselves and to every one that fair is foul and foul is fair;
for foul is useful and fair is not. Avarice and usury and precau-
tion must be our gods for a little longer still. For only they can
lead us out of the tunnel of economic necessity into daylight."

With this statement Keynes wanted to stress that in his
time the era of poverty and scarcity was not over yet. In this
he was right, of course, but his anticipation that poverty and
scarcity will be over in a few decades was naive and objection-

able. It was naive, because it was based on the assumption that the world population was shortly going to level off just above the two billion mark reached in 1930. On the contrary it is well known that the population explosion has gone on and that poverty and scarcity — as well as exhaustion of certain natural resources — are getting worse, at least for one billion humans.

Keynes' statement is also objectionable, because theorizing and justifying any kind of foulness on the basis that it is inevitable, may contribute to produce even more injustice. The more so — the more the theoretician who provides the justification is authoritative.

Keynes' opinion is objectionable, but perhaps too many objections have been raised against it out of context. In fact in the same essay Keynes talks about the possible alternative goals and values, which will be pursued by the majority of people once they get rid of the more pressing economic needs. He concluded that the rich of his time — who are already rid of these needs — have failed disastrously to solve this problem of values and goals, as they dedicate time and energies to silly and futile activities or interests. We can conclude — as I shall indicate more fully in Chapter 12 — that the really important thing is a cultural revolution which will change values and goals — even if Keynes did not go so far explicitly.

We all know that innovation has been the most significant trait of technology at least in the last 150 years. In every economics textbook we find statements to the effect that technological innovation more than offsets the consequences of diminishing returns. In the past, in fact, the law of diminishing returns has been visible only over the short term, whereas it has no validity over the long term.

We do not know very well the mechanisms of applicative innovation, through which scientific discoveries find their productive use in technology. There are many different opinions concerning the nature and the genesis of these mechanisms. There are some who contend that the main function of technical innovation is to strengthen the power of capital over labor. Technological innovation, then, would be motivated by political, rather than economic, reasons and the means through which it could be used to subdue the workers are:

- use of innovation in data processing, which permits to establish more stringent controls and checks
- fragmentation of workers' groups, obtained by reshuffling them frequently, following ever-changing centralization or decentralization needs or the introduction of new automated technologies
- forced obsolescence — and consequently less bargaining power — of less qualified workers, whose functions are carried out by new automatic machines.

According to others even technological innovations intended to improve working conditions and, integrated in job enrichment programs, have the real aim of wetting the powders of the workers' fights to obtain higher salaries and lower productivity.

As we shall see in the next chapter, there are explanations of technological innovation mechanisms, which are completely different from those referred to above, and according to which technological innovation — or its lack — is the most important factor behind economic cycles.

I do not agree with the point of view, represented as necessary by some, according to which we will have true alternatives to technology and productive organization (as they have been established in industrialized countries), only after the whole political and socio-economic structure of society is deeply changed by a radical revolutionary process. In order to accept it we should also believe in the possibility of laying out the plan of a revolution and then of implementing it with a revolution which proceeds just as it has been planned. Many case histories — from the French to the Russian revolution — prove that the reverse is true: the type of regime and of socio-economic situation after a revolution bears almost no relationship to the plans that had been formulated before. In many cases too it happens that: *plus ça change, plus c'est la même chose.*

As I noted talking about Schumacher's reasonable proposals, the burden of designing modest technologies is indeed heavy. A first pitfall to be avoided is the one of generic statements. We can well say that the majority of workers should find the new technologies help them to avoid alienation and to strengthen feelings of solidarity and cooperation. This statement is useless, though, unless we also explain clearly and with concrete examples how these goals should and could be pursued.

We often hear or read in the newspapers that alienation could be eliminated from production work if: oppressive controls were decreased (more on this in Chapter 8, p. 96); organizations were made simpler; production and also management activities were decentralized; training processes were made less formal and uniform. The fact that we can list these alleged ills to be eliminated does not mean we can be sure that the situation prevailing after their elimination would be acceptable to the workers. We cannot be sure either that it would permit us to achieve certain productivity levels, nor certain living standards or *per capita* income. This is not surprising. In fact if we want to define a completely new socio-economic and technological situation, we have to supply the equivalent of the design of a large and complex system — different from any other system previously realized.

It is well known that there are no general standardized procedures for designing large new systems. Before we begin to use formalized procedures of any type, we must make an effort of imagination and try to conceive a model of a reality which is complex and different from any we have known. Anybody who makes proposals for new and more or less utopian alternative technologies, should do just that: imagine all the implications and consequences. It is not an easy task nor one that can be taken care of on the basis of a first simple and enlightening intuition. Intuitions are necessary, but they have to be analyzed carefully and they have to be followed by experiments. We should also remember that small scale experiments do not always supply results which can be significantly extrapolated to larger scale applications. After the intuitions, we have to formulate hypotheses which will be then verified or falsified by practical experience.

Complex decisions which tend to innovate socio-economic systems, can be counterintuitive, as originally suggested by Jay W. Forrester. A good case in point is to be found in a project prepared by the Long Range Intelligence Division of the British Post Office ("Long Range Social Forecasts: Working from Home"; Long Range Intelligence Bulletin 2, published by Post Office Telecommunications, July 1974). The project analyzes the reasonable hypothesis of replacing massively personal travel and displacements by telecommunication services provided by integrated networks having much better levels of performance than present day ones .

The study follows all the good rules of the trade. It includes:

— appropriately disaggregated demographic projections
— projections of telephone traffic, based on present utilization types (voice, alpha-numeric data, facsimile)
— economic forecasts of *per capita* income and socio-economic structure of the United Kingdom
— forecasts on the size of bureaucratic and tertiary chores in general to the year 2001.

The study concludes that by the year 2001, 8 million employees (about 27% of the active population) of industrial and commercial companies as well as of government, local authorities and other public corporations, will be able to work from home.

Of course for this to be possible, these white collar employees will have to be connected with each other and to some central office not only by telephone, but also with wide band channels carrying signals for teleprinter, facsimile, data processing terminal, multiple telephone conference and, possibly, videotelephone or slow scan TV.

The replacement of the trips of employees to their offices by telecommunications and work carried out from home, should provide the following advantages:

— saving of time previously spent in commuting
— savings of energy in transportation systems
— reduction in number of vehicles used and in their wear
— reduction of pollution
— savings in initial investment and running costs for centralized facilities.

The study indicates that these advantages carry more weight than the disadvantages like excessive isolation and drawbacks to family life caused by the work from home. We could conclude, then, that the Post Office project may represent a significant step towards decentralization, humanization of work, energy saving, elimination of waste and increase in efficiency. It is not so: not only for socio-psychological difficulties, but because of much more basic technical and organizational reasons.

This general plan of work from home would achieve only an apparent decentralization. All the communications which at present take place on many parallel and redundant channels — admittedly at the expense of displacements and expenses — in the new system would all go through a single communication system. Consequently the whole of society: industry, commerce, government, would become much more vulnerable. Every outfit in every sector would depend critically on the level of service of the centralized telecommunications system. In turn this level of service is determined by the inherent stability and efficiency of the network, technical faults, congestion due to an excess of demand over capacity, and finally, by possible interferences of other systems — and notably the electric power distribution system. If the centralized communications network were to stop, everything else would stop: banks, offices, ministries and then gradually management centers, plants, and all kinds of systems. It would be difficult to rig up alternative operation modes for all these outfits as their employees would not even have a place where to *go* and work: they would not even know how to find the premises of their employers.

I have described in detail the complications that would arise if large numbers of people were working from home to illustrate that it is not enough to affirm the desirability of general criteria — like decentralization. We must also try to look farther ahead for possible negative consequences.

It is not enough, either, to state that we should: use less natural resources; avoid damaging the environment or societal structures; adapt the new technologies to the lowest social and educational levels. It is not enough to pinpoint a single feature of any new proposed technology like certain types of organic agriculture, certain recycling processes, certain balances between manual and intellectual work. When these individual features or provisions are reasonable, they can be incorporated in existing production and technological structures without any need of radical and sweeping changes of the whole structure of industrial production. Industrial and public decision makers do not adopt readily these minor and reasonable changes, because of their well known inertia and resistance to innovation.

We can well agree that technological innovation — its motivations and consequences, interactions between ideology and technology, long term planning of new technologies, are all vital and important questions. However, practicing economists, ivory tower economists, industrialists, union officials and politicians give to these same questions a quite low priority. We cannot ignore the priorities accepted and to a certain extent acted upon by all the categories of people I have just quoted. High priority items are well known to be:

- unemployment and growth of employment levels
- inflation and purchasing power
- balance of payments of any country we consider towards other countries
- gross national product
- rate of increase of the money supply.

There is a consensus that these are the true problems of society and that the knowledge of their mechanisms is quite objective and neutral (as far as it goes) and untouched by ideological taint. These problems are deeply felt both in industrialized countries and in less developed countries. How would they be affected by the introduction of innovative modest technologies? The conventional wisdom would answer that they would hardly be affected at all: the solutions are to be found elsewhere. If this were true, we could look forward to the future in a much happier frame of mind. We could also anticipate that the solutions to these serious problems are imminent and we could argue that after these solutions have been implemented, decision makers will be more readily available to consider seriously new alternative technologies. Until the more pressing problems have been solved, decision makers will be interested in alternative technologies only if someone can prove plausibly that they are adequate for solving the immediate problems of unemployment, inflation and so on.

All the high priority items I have listed above are interdependent. If one changes — or if we succeed in changing one of them forcibly, hopefully believing we are improving the situation — most of the others change too. The mechanisms of this interdependence are not simple ones.

Various schools of thought have developed to provide explanations of these mechanisms. Their views are in profound disagreement. The controversies in which they engage tend to remind us of the older controversies among philosophical schools.

Let us try now to analyze certain mechanisms the existence of which is almost generally accepted in Western type mixed economies.

Consider first the interdependence tie between unemployment rate (computed on the active population), inflation (or yearly average rate of price increases) and annual rate of increase of salaries. If we draw a diagram of the yearly rate of inflation plotted against unemployment rates prevailing at the same time, we should find that it has approximately the shape of a hyperbole. This is known as Phillips' curve (named after A. W. Phillips of the London School of Economics). For example in the Sixties in the United States the Phillips curve could appear roughly as indicated in the figure below

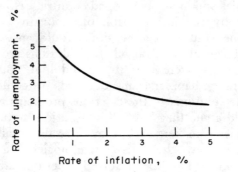

The three following situations would then be typical of the mechanism described by the curve:

unemployment rate (%)	inflation rate (%)
1.8	5
3	2
5	0.5

These data mirror reality in a rather imprecise way. It probably never happened during those years that inflation was down to 0.5% and that simultaneously 5% of the active population was unemployed. It could be argued plausibly, though, that this situation could have been achieved and even that with a somewhat higher unemployment rate, all prices would have stopped increasing altogether.

In the Sixties the average productivity of labor in the United States was growing at a fairly constant rate. Roughly productivity increased by 3% every year which would have permitted salaries to grow on the average 3% more than the inflation rate. Consequently the purchasing power of salaried workers could have grown exactly in the same proportion of productivity. With an inflation rate of 5%, salaries would have grown by 8% per year. With inflation rates of 2% or 0.5%, salaries could have grown on the average of 5% or 3.5%.

This is ancient history by now. In the late Seventies the Phillips curves for the United States and for the majority of European countries appear as very short segments, which stand no chance of crossing one of the coordinate axes in the figure on the previous page. If they could cross the abscissae axis, it would mean that full employment has been achieved. If they crossed the ordinate vertical axis, it would mean that prices are absolutely constant.

For the majority of countries, inflation rates have been hovering around 10%. Italy and England have had rates of more than 20%, they have done better in 1978, but in 1979 Italy is headed again towards very high inflation.

A remarkable exception is Switzerland, where the inflation rate was 10% in 1974, but came down very steeply to 6% in 1975 and then plummeted to 1.9% in 1976 and to just above 1% thereafter. This was obtained by a drastic tightening of the money supply.

In the meanwhile, unemployment has been varying between 5 and 10% for most countries. Switzerland is again a remarkable exception with practically zero unemployment. This result, though, was obtained only by sending back 185,000 foreign workers to their countries of origin. On a total working population of about 2.6 million, these 185,000 represented about 7%. In other words the Swiss managed to export unemployment: getting rid of this hefty problem represented a good portion of the Swiss solution.

One could be tempted to argue simplistically that the Swiss fare better than practically all other countries, because they have used fiscal and monetary interventions adequate to achieve stability. The Swiss were saved, then, because they followed the advice of neoclassic economists, e.g. to the effect of the Samuelson quote on page ix. This may well be part of the truth. Another part is that the Swiss economy is small enough that it can prosper by exporting unemployment — since in absolute numbers it sends back not very many workers to each country. It can prosper with the Swiss franc considerably over-valued with respect to other currencies, because Swiss goods, even if overpriced, are of high enough quality to secure a small share of the international market, which again is quite enough for the size of Swiss industry.

The mechanisms tying unemployment to inflation and to salary increases are not as rigid nor as clearly understood as some theoreticians had been maintaining. In the late Sixties and in the Seventies the rate of salary increases has been quite high and, particularly in Europe, it has not been accompanied by a proportional increase in productivity. Stabilization mechanisms did not work. One of the most important of these mechanisms should have been the control over the yearly rate of increase of liquidity. The increase of liquidity influences investment levels and, consequently, also unemployment and inflation rates.

The yearly rate of increase of liquidity is determined by national central banks. Another legend — accepted by many as true — is that the yearly rate of increase of liquidity is simply 2% more than the inflation rate. If this were true, it would be enough to increase the money supply of just 2% per year, to have zero inflation. But for this to happen it would be necessary for the rate of increase of salaries to follow the changes in the other variables, rather than be determined by collective agreements between unions and industry. Historically these agreements have often been incompatible with any reasonable planning of inflation and of unemployment.

Towards the end of 1976, the economists Robert E. Lucas of the University of Chicago, and Neil Wallace and Thomas J. Sargent of the University of Minnesota, have come up with their theory of rational expectations. According to them, monetary and fiscal interventions made by governments can only influence the inflation rate, but not employment and productivity. This is because businessmen have learnt to anticipate any government intervention and, therefore, to discount them in advance and to neutralize them.

Let us suppose that during a recession phase, the government decides to cut taxes to people or corporations who make new investments. Let us suppose also that this government is success-

ful: investments soar, the recession vanishes — economy flouri-
shes again. If this sequence of events is repeated a certain
number of times, investors understand the mechanism and they
begin to behave differently, in subsequent occasions. When a
new recession begins to loom ahead, they stop to invest much
more drastically than before, because they are waiting once
again for the government to announce another tax cut. Consequently this type of government policy may be used to fight
the downward slopes of economic cycles for a certain time.
Later the very fact that businessmen rationally expect, and
consequently discount, future government interventions, represents a factor which contributes to make the downward
slopes of economic cycles even steeper and more precipitous.

Something similar happens when a government increases the
money supply in order to avoid a recession which looms ahead
but does not exist yet. The first few times government interventions like this are tried, they succeed in stimulating production and in preventing the recession. Later people realize that
they have overspent and overborrowed and the next time the
money supply is increased, real output does not go up — it is
just prices that do.

We cannot envisage seriously any massive attempt to devise
government policies intended to surprise the public in general
and businessmen in particular. The only solution — according
to Lucas, Wallace and Sargent — is to define and declare a clear
policy of modest growth of the money supply — and then to
adhere strictly to it. At the same time long term agreements or
peace pacts with workers' unions should stabilize salary levels.

Apart from Switzerland, this is the policy chosen by the
Federal Republic of Germany and, to a certain extent, by the
United States. The inflation rates of these three countries have
been:

	1974	1975	1976	1977	1978
United States	11	9	5.9	6.5	7.7
West Germany	7	6	4.5	3.9	2.6
Switzerland	10	6	1.9	1.3	1.1

If the policies adopted by these three countries are not pursued also by other countries, the latter will probably be heading towards unmanageable situations. Inflationary policies have no future, when the rates of exchange between currencies are flexible.

And yet it is doubtful whether these reasonable policies will be adopted. It is also doubtful whether these latest theories advanced to explain the complex mechanisms of economic interactions will stand the test of being compared with future events. These theories, in fact, have not been proved in any satisfactory quantitative sense. It is highly likely that in future they will have to be deeply revised.

The present situation is certainly critical. We cannot hope that stagnation and inflation will just vanish and will be replaced by a period of prosperity and boom — without anybody really knowing why. Before we begin to get a consistent flow of good news, we will have had to solve many problems: energy, justice in the distribution of resources, conservation and recycling of resources, defining the policies which can guarantee socio-economic equilibrium.

Some of these solutions will be provided by science and technology, which — for some reason — appear to be under suspicion particularly in difficult economic periods.

We have seen that economic theories and explanations — neutral or not — may not claim to provide objective and final explanations of socio-economic phenomena. On the other hand there are important clues to the effect that the most important cause of economic cycles is the lack of applicative innovation. This suspicion concerning the very channels that link science to technology, is so serious that I have dedicated the next chapter to its discussion.

CHAPTER 6

Lack of Innovation as a Cause of Economic Crisis

IF a company tries to introduce a new product in a new market, its chances of success are one in twenty. If it tries to introduce an old and proved product in a new market, the chances are better: one in four. A new product entering an old well known market, has one chance in two. Finally if a company tries to introduce in an old market, an old product already marketed successfully by other companies — that is a "me-too" product — then the probability of success is almost 50%.

These approximate probabilities have been evaluated in 1975 by A. T. Kearney, Inc., an American firm of management consultants. The evaluation mirrors a very conservative attitude of American business. Prudent conservatism has been so common in recent years that *Business Week* devoted the cover story of the February 16, 1976 issue to the breakdown of U.S. innovation.

Historically, the average American companies devote 9% of their yearly billings to research and development. The distribution is not uniform by a long shot. Aerospace companies spend 18% of their billings on research and development — but the large majority of this effort is financed directly by the Government for military or space purposes. All other types of industries on average are below 9%, even though individual innovative companies may often represent remarkable exceptions. The pharmaceutical industry invests an average of 8% of sales in research and development; automotive and chemical industries are at 3%, oil companies are at 0.5% and steel companies are last with only 0.3% of billings.

In the United States in the Seventies, military and even more space exploration programs have been drastically reduced. This has been one of the major factors in reducing the absolute value of investment in research and development. According to Richard Atkinson, director of the National Science Foundation, between 1969 and 1979 the number of scientists and engineers in U.S. industrial research and development has declined by 13%. Between 1971 and 1976, the number of U.S. patents issued to American corporations dropped by about 20%. And yet these are not the worst signs to be seen.

A more serious cause of worry is to be found in the new character of innovations. These are represented less and less by really new applications of scientific discoveries to the technological field. More and more often innovations are just extensions of the state of the art or commercial innovations — like the introduction of known products in new markets or changes in the outward appearance of traditional products.

The percentages of yearly sales devoted to investment in research and development as given on the previous page, indicate that at present, innovation is higher in the fields of electronics, computers and instrumentation. Real innovation is lagging in the automotive, chemical, steel and paper industries.

The causes of this slowdown have been variously attributed to purely economic or financial factors and also to excessive government regulations. Other plausible factors are:

- simultaneous increased sophistication of the market's demand and more stringent quality, safety and anti-pollution standards. Consequently design and experimentation costs soar and act as a deterrent to most innovative decisions
- competition is stiffer than in the past and consequently the average life of products is now much shorter. In 1967, the average life of products was of about 7 years, whereas in 1979 it appears to be only slightly more than 4 years
- as the size of companies and the scale of production both grow, the absolute value of risks also increases. At the

same time investments aimed at researching and finding solutions for problems which are increasingly complex, reach levels which are so high as to bring them out of range of individual companies.

Most people who look at these facts tend to worry that the lag — or the breakdown — of innovation may clamp down on the rate at which Western economies will grow in the future. They worry that public opinion will not accept the low rates of growth. Some worry that their own country will lag technologically with respect to one or more other countries.

Hardly anybody seems to be worrying that the lack of innovation may have much deeper effects: not only of preventing growth, but also of leading the economy towards a depression much worse than all those we have experienced since World War Two.

A young German economist, Gerhard Mensch, suggests just that in a book he published in 1975 on the technological stalemate (Gerhard Mensch, *Das Technologische Patt,* Umschau Verlag, Frankfurt a.M., 1975). The idea that the lack of innovation may cause economic crises was suggested initially by J. A. Schumpeter. Mensch has added now a very detailed and significant documentation as well as an interesting interpretation of the events of the last few decades.

Mensch starts out describing the phases of an industrial economy: from expansion and boom to recession, then to depression and to the subsequent take-off. During the expansion phase growing incomes give strength to the market for consumer goods. Demand goes up continuously and creates a seller's market. Manufacturers have very fat backlogs, which permit them to plan their future production as well as investments. They can dictate their conditions to buyers, who are so many and so hungry to accept them and to go on buying. Manufacturers employ part of their increasing profits to build bigger and bigger production plants, so they can achieve economies of scale. Then they need larger and larger markets so they can exploit adequately the new plants. After a certain point manufacturers can continue to expand only if they attack foreign markets.

Bur foreign manufacturers are playing the same game. Competition becomes harsher and at first prices stop going up and then tend to fall. The difference in quality between the products of different manufacturers becomes smaller and smaller, also because it is more advantageous to introduce marginal and superficial improvements of products, rather than real innovations. Mensch calls these superficial improvements "Schein-innovationen": the term fits rather well the phenomena which have taken place in the United States and to which I was referring above.

The harsher competition causes profits to decrease sharply: we go to recession and, gradually, to depression. Demand plummets, unemployment goes up and the meagre returns offered by industry do not attract fresh capital. Liquidity may be high but new investments are low. A technological stalemate may be said to have occurred: industry continues to produce goods intended to satisfy traditional demand, which has levelled off, but does not succeed in creating new demand. This could be done only after new fields of industrial activity have been opened up.

Sequences of events similar to those just described have taken place in the past. Phases of economic and industrial stagnation have occurred in 1814–28, 1870–86, 1929–39 – that is roughly every 50 years. Incidentally a business cycle period of 50 years had been suggested on a purely empirical basis in the Twenties by the Soviet economist N. D. Kondratieff. His theories have not been accepted too widely in Russia, but they have had a considerable revival in the West, as apparently they can be used to forecast with fair accuracy the price variations of raw materials. The mechanisms suggested by Mensch could probably supply a rational basis and justification for the regularities recorded empirically by Kondratieff. Another interesting confirmation of Kondratieff's interpretations has been given by the mathematical model of the United States economy – the Systems Dynamics National Model – implemented on a computer by J. W. Forrester, famous for having conceived the systems dynamics computerized model on which the Limits to Growth report to the Club of Rome was originally based.

Mensch suggests, then, that the lack of industrial innovation during the boom and even at the beginning of recession — when business goes on exploiting the fat seller's markets — is the very cause of recession, first, and then of depression. Only when industry recurs again to innovation — as a last resort against the prevalent economic crisis, which cannot be fought by any other means — and finds applications for a large number of scientific inventions, which had been left unused in their merely potential state, then the economy can find its way out of the depression. At the lowest point of depression, innovation begins again and a new economic take-off is experienced.

The technological stalemate is, then, caused by the fact that theoretically available inventions are not put into practice on an industrial scale and — in turn — a new start of applicative innovation is the cure for technological stalemate and for economic crisis.

We can conclude that presumably economic crises would not take place if industrialists continued to introduce relevant innovations also during periods of boom and prosperity. Innovations are relevant, in this context, when they open up new virgin territories to industry. This happened for example: with steam engines after 1830, with the chemical and the electrical industry after 1880 and, after 1940, with the developments of electronics, telecommunications, electronic computers, nuclear and aerospace engineering.

People in business circles normally reject this type of explanation in favor of the so called echo theory. According to them, applicative innovations are just an echo of scientific inventions or discoveries. Innovation follows invention with a brief and constant lag. If industry fails to innovate, it means that in the immediately previous years scientific inventions have been scarce. The alleged habit of industry of exploiting as far as possible any period of prosperity, trying to realize economies of scale and introducing only cheap and superficial innovations, would not be a reprehensible omission. It would be the only available way — since science and basic research are not offering any new applicative possibility.

Mensch has recorded and processed data proving that the echo theory is false. In fact, basic scientific inventions present no discontinuity in time. Mensch has analyzed many different fields — from chemistry to electricity, from mechanics to electronics — and he has found that in each field new important scientific discoveries or inventions crop up with a frequency which is rarely less than two, or more than five per decade. On the contrary the frequency of applicative innovations is very low (one every ten years or less) during boom periods and goes up to ten or more per decade just at the end of depression periods.

Let us look, for example, at applicative innovations in the field of electrical engineering and of chemistry. These began to appear on a large enough scale for the first time between 1881 and 1890: but — during that same decade — it seems that no major invention has been made in either field.

Between 1881 and 1890 industry had produced for the first time on a large scale hydraulic turbines, telephones, electric heating, electric cables, steam turbines, transformers, electric welding and electric energy meters. These eight applicative innovations were derived from basic inventions made, on the average, 40 years before. The oldest was the manufacturing of electric cables, invented in 1820. The most recent invention was electric heating, which dated from 1859.

In the field of chemistry, ten applicative innovations were made during the same decade. They were production of iodoform, chloroform, veronal, antipyrin, chinolin, cocaine, aluminum, artificial silk, fertilizer and electrolysis. The corresponding inventions had been made on the average fifty years before. The feasibility of electrolysis had been demonstrated in 1789. The invention which had been transferred more quickly to practical application was artificial silk, which dated back to 1857 and was produced on an industrial scale 33 years later.

In any boom period there is, then, a reserve of potentially usable inventions, which are not exploited, as inertia makes for the exploitation of products which are easier, safer and more profitable over the short term. For example, only after the crisis of the early Thirties did available inventions begin to be exploited one after the other, such as hydraulic couplings, diesel locomotives, color photography, magnetic recorders, penicillin, gyrocompass, neoprene, etc.

Mensch maintains — and he is not the only one — that Keynesian recipes intended to eliminate unemployment by means of public investment and of increasing deficit spending on the part of governments, often fail to achieve their goals. He gives the example of the very scarce effect made on the German economy by the West German public investments in 1967. These investments were massive — more than $3 billion in less than one year. They were concentrated, however, in traditional fields (public works, etc.) and therefore, they were doomed to fail. Only if investments are concentrated in really innovative sectors, will they represent a real energetic remedy. On the other hand the innovative and pioneering programs of the Pentagon, of NASA and of the Atomic Energy Commission have produced relatively scarce spin-offs for American industry. This indicates that even innovation is not enough in itself — without adequate plans and strategies.

It is a commonly accepted viewpoint that the tempo of scientific and technological progress has been accelerating continuously and is still accelerating, also as regards transfers from scientific invention to technological innovation. This is a half truth: let us see why.

It is actually true that scientific progress is developing at an increasing speed. The number of pure scientists, the number of published scientific papers, the investments made in science and, presumably, the results obtained are doubling every 10 to 15 years.

Some figures also seem to indicate that the time necessary for proceeding from scientific invention to technological innovation gets shorter and shorter. This time interval was

85 years for steam engines (1769–1854), 56 years for the telephone (1820–1876), 35 years for radio (1867–1902), 15 years for radar (1925–1940) and only 5 years for transistors (1948–1953). Here we could argue that transistors have not really opened a new field to industry and to the economy — they have replaced much more advantageously the performance already provided by electronic tubes. Steam engines and telephones have modified industry and the economy much more. Again, the counter argument here is that the real transistor (or silicon) revolution has not arrived yet. It will arrive with the imminent full impact of VLSI (Very Large Scale Integration), bringing in millions of microprocessors, with infinite new functions and applications — many of which are yet to be made available and even to be defined.

The time interval for technological transfer from invention to innovation is decreasing mainly for apparent innovations. The very fact that in this context we would list transistors among apparent innovations, explains the real meaning and the limits of this type of categorization.

If we want to corroborate the theory that economic crises are caused by the lack of innovation, we should supply a list of important inventions which have not yet led to practical innovations in the late Seventies. This list could explain the genesis of the economic crisis which has begun with stagflation and which should continue — according to the theory — well into the mid Eighties, with a new period of prosperity to begin in the early Nineties.

If we accept the estimate of 35 years for the time interval between invention and innovation in the case of radio, this means that we consider J. C. Maxwell's theory of the electromagnetic field as the basic invention. Actually the practical laboratory demonstration of the existence of electromagnetic waves was provided by Hertz in 1888. Using the same criterion, we can say then that hydrogen bombs, theoretical and experimental results of magneto-hydrodynamics and of laser represent the inventions which are prerequisites to nuclear fusion energy production. This would certainly be an innovation that would open up a new industrial field, that would supply practically unlimited and clean (i.e. almost free of radioactive waste) energy — solving present predicaments.

Apart from nuclear fusion energy, there are many other methods of energy production which are well known and proven, but applied only marginally. They are so important that the next chapter is devoted to their description.

In the field of communications, again, laser technology is available — but only marginally applied. Holography invented and proved in the early Fifties, has had next to no application yet.

The theory that lack of innovation is responsible for economic crises is, at least, quite plausible. To give a concrete idea of the impact of a single applied invention, let us consider just xerography. In less than twenty years this innovation has led to the creation of an industry with a volume of almost $5 billion and 150,000 employees — just in the United States. Apart from the impact of the availability of xerocopies on the organization and efficiency of industry in general, consider that just 6 new industries of this importance would create almost one million new jobs, which would represent a major factor of economic prosperity.

Another invention — if we can call it an invention — that has not been applied significantly and widely enough, is systems engineering. The modern theoretical advances and new procedures of this discipline would allow us to design and to run large technological and socio-economic systems much better than we are doing now. In this way we would also be able to avoid the known risks of multiple congestive crises due to the degradation of large systems.

Even the passage from invention to innovation is a complex process, for the implementation and optimization of which systems analysis should be used in a massive way.

CHAPTER 7

How to be Energetically Modest

"TO the Honorable Members of the Chamber of Deputies:

We are subjected to the intolerable competition of a foreign rival, who appears to enjoy such superior facilities for the production of light that he can inundate our national market at fabulously reduced prices. In fact, as soon as this competitor appears, our sales stop altogether, all the consumers go to him and an entire sector of French industry . . . is suddenly hit by the most complete stagnation. This rival is no other than the sun . . . . We ask you to pass a law ordering to shut up all windows, dormer-windows, casements, skylights — in a word all openings, holes or fissures through which the light of the sun usually gets into our homes — to the prejudice of the fine manufactures, which we flatter ourselves we have given to our country."

"Petition of candle-makers, lamp manufacturers, producers of oil, alcohol and in general of anything which pertains to lighting."

This satirical piece was published in 1881 by the French free-trade economist, and member of the Chamber of Deputies, F. Bastiat in his pamphlet *Sophismes Economiques*. Bastiat wanted to ridicule the protectionist policies of the French government of his time. He goes on — seriously — to maintain that blocking off sunlight, which is free, would be just about the same as preventing the entry into France by means of very

62

stiff customs tariffs, of foreign goods sold by their manufacturers at much lower prices than those prevailing in France.

Bastiat's piece is openly paradoxical, but all the same it
looks as if his advice has been taken quite seriously in a number
of countries. In fact the sun sends over to earth not only
light, but also heat — that is: energy. We have been talking
about the energy crisis for years. We have been talking — but
just talking — about energy conservation. We have begun —
but just begun — to evaluate the energy consumption necessary
for the production of different materials and for manufacturing
different objects. And yet the use of solar energy is still
marginal, even in countries which are near the equator, where
the solar energy obtainable per square meter is highest.

Possible uses of solar energy come in all sizes.

There is a very long term project for exploiting solar energy
which is gigantic. The idea is to close the Red Sea at Bab al
Mandab with a dam, which would be 15 km long and in certain
points 1 km deep. After the dam is completed, the sun would
cause the water in the Red Sea to evaporate and its level to go
down — while the level of the Indian Ocean would not change,
of course. After a few dozen years, the head — or difference
between the two levels — will be such that it will be possible
to let Ocean water flow into the Red Sea producing appreciable
amounts of energy. The level of the Red Sea would continue
to go down, because evaporation is so massive. In about 400
years the situation would become stable. The head would be
400 m and the water of the Indian Ocean flowing back into the
Red Sea would produce many thousand megawatts, and then
would evaporate again, keeping the level of the Red Sea constant.
It would also be necessary, of course, to close the Suez canal.

Apart from the disadvantage of eliminating an important
sea route and the very long waiting time before any energy
could be produced — the feasibility of this truly pharaonic project would be difficult to prove. In order to appreciate this difficulty, think of the unexpected environmental and agricultural
consequences of a much smaller and conventional project like
the Aswan dam.

Fiat has built and installed in Southern Italy a 1 MW solar power station, with mirrors concentrating sun rays on a boiler which produces steam, exploited in a steam turbine. In the United States the Aerospace Corporation has designed, but not built, similar and much bigger solar power stations. These would have an installed power of many hundred megawatts and their collectors would cover an area of many square kilometers.

These large scale applications of solar energy cannot be readily implemented because of the many existing technical difficulties which have not been solved yet and because they present a very marginal cost/benefit picture. On the contrary small scale applications of solar energy are well proven and could be adopted readily. These are low temperature applications: mainly heating of water for domestic use and space heating. The diffusion of the small solar panels, though, is quite slow — because of inertia and lack of innovative spirit, but mainly for lack of motivation.

The latter factor is probably the most important. In Israel the latitude is low and innovative spirit is high. Consequently between 1964 and 1974 quite a few hundred thousand solar panels were installed for heating water in homes, offices and plants. The water heated in the panels is stored in thermically insulated reservoirs, which are equipped with a thermostat. During cloudy days or when too much hot water is used, the thermostat switches on automatically an electric heater. In the mid Seventies in very many installations any maintenance of the panels, including the periodic cleaning of their external double glass plates, had been interrupted. Consequently very little solar energy seeped into the water, which was heated almost exclusively by electricity. Life was made a little easier for the owners of the panels — and they spent a bit more for electricity. This did not worry them because electric energy tariffs had not been brought up to date and were ridiculously low.

This is the case in most countries. In Italy the situation is particularly warped. In 1929 the average price for one kilowatt hour was 2 lire; in 1979 it is 45 lire. The unit price has increased 22.5 times — whereas during the same fifty years the average increase of the price indexes was almost 300 times. This unbalance is partly due to the fact that 50 years ago the great majority of electricity in Italy was produced by private monopolies, who pushed prices up and quantities down, and also, of course, by technological innovation. On the other hand it is evident that prices of electric energy to consumers are much too low in the late Seventies. One kilowatt hour sells for as little as 3 U.S. cents in Sweden, and 5.5 cents in Italy. In 1978 the average price to the ultimate customers of one kilowatt hour in the U.S. was 3.5 cents. The order of magnitude is the same in all these countries. Ironically large industrial users pay a lot less for their kilowatt hour (as little as one or two cents). As I shall try to prove in Chapter 9, this price structure is wholly artificial. It lures consumers into choices which are only apparently rational and which contribute, instead, to create risky and disadvantageous conditions for the whole community.

While unit prices for other sources of power — like electricity — are kept unduly low, solar energy is at a disadvantage, because at present installation costs are very high. This is due to the fact that existing homes and buildings were designed to use other forms of energy (electricity, gasoil or natural gas heating). Consequently they have to be retrofitted in order to equip them with solar heating systems. Retrofitting often involves masonry work and makes installation much more expensive than would be the case if the buildings had been designed initially for solar energy. All these difficulties have made for a scarce diffusion of solar energy, which has entailed unit prices of equipment to stay at high levels. At the same time labor costs for installations are also high, since there are not very many technicians trained to carry out these jobs.

On top of all these negative factors there is a time factor which is also negative. If you want to equip your home with solar heating for water and space, you have to pay now your high installation and retrofitting costs — your savings, instead, are way off in the future: you have to wait 4 to 7 years for them, before you have amortized your initial costs. This does a lot to stave off individuals from going solar. In fact it is typical that individuals perceive only money saving — in the present — rather than energy saving, which affects them through indirect and delayed actions. Energy saving should be perceived by public decision makers: by governments and by elected representatives. They do not seem to be perceiving the need for energy saving at all.

In May 1979, the 20 member governments of the International Energy Agency (all of the major Western oil-importing countries except France) decided jointly that they would try to cut their oil consumption by 5%. In view of the recent Iranian crisis and the soaring OPEC pricing, this decision appears as ludicrously inadequate. The only statesman who appears to be really sensitive to the oil crisis is President Carter — but he has not managed to get the support of the U.S. Congress nor of U.S. public opinion.

In the absence of adequate governmental policies, we might place our hopes on some other innovative breakthrough. This could be the case of the direct conversion of solar energy into electricity by means of photovoltaic cells. This conversion is perfectly feasible. Operational units have been installed on a multitude of space vehicles and also on remote inaccessible locations on the earth's surface. The trouble is that photovoltaic conversion requires an initial investment in power generating equipment which, at best, is hundreds of times higher than the investment necessary for any other form of generation (nuclear, hydroelectric, thermal). This factor is decisive enough and, on top of it, conversion efficiency is quite low (at present around 10%, whereas the theoretical maximum should be about 20%).

Experts think that this state of affairs will not change in the foreseeable future. Large scale production of electricity from photovoltaic cells appears, then, to be utopian. On the other hand, experts have frequently erred in the past because of excessive caution — hardly ever because of excessive optimism and imagination. Let us examine quickly what would happen if the unit cost of photovoltaic cells could be lowered considerably and their efficiency could be brought up to, say, 15%.

The first problem to be solved is the availability of adequate areas. A power station of a few hundred megawatts would occupy quite a few square kilometers.

Norbert Weyss of the International Institute for Applied Systems Analysis (IIASA, in Schloss Laxenburg, Austria) has suggested that the huge surfaces of photovoltaic cells could be installed on floats covering the surfaces of barrage and dam lakes. The electric power generated by the photovoltaic cells would be of the same order of magnitude as the power produced by the hydroelectric plant. The water of the lake would easily provide cooling for the 85% of the energy which goes into heat.

Another interesting possibility would be to build many smaller photovoltaic power stations. These could be installed on agricultural land which is not very fertile and which has been abandoned — as has been the case so often in Europe, especially in hilly ground. The electric energy produced could go into the electric grid or it could be supplied to local users or it could be used for producing hydrogen — the energy vector of the future according to some. The large amounts of waste heat produced by the photovoltaic cells could be used for hothouses, so these abandoned areas would be reclaimed for a high yield specialized agricultural production.

Photovoltaic power is not for today, but it will probably supply a portion of tomorrow's solutions. When this happens, it will be usable in small as well as in large power stations.

Wind power is available now in the form of modern high efficiency windmills with an installed power of a few kilowatts up to hundreds of kilowatts. It can be used directly for pumping water — as in the traditional agricultural installations — or to produce electricity. The snag is that wind power cannot be used when the wind is too slow — obviously — and again it cannot be used when the wind is too strong, otherwise the frame supporting the wheel or blades would have to be too massive and expensive. A special application of wind power would be to a new breed of large cargo sailboats. There are designs to build them up to tens of thousand tons. Of course they would have auxiliary engines and all the sails maneuvering would be carried out by means of mechanical and automatic devices. The savings in fuel would be remarkable.

Another alternative source, open to innovation on a large scale and also on a small scale, is the production of hydrocarbons from renewable resources. Fifteen per cent of the automotive fuel used in Brazil is alcohol, produced from the fermentation of sugar cane and manioc. Many different kinds of agricultural waste can be recycled for producing alcohol. If the waste has a high sugar content, then it can be fermented and distilled. If the waste has a high cellulose content, first it has to be hydrolized with diluted acids and then it can be fermented and distilled. The corresponding technology has been known for dozens of years and it was used by many countries (including the United States) during World War Two. Some contemporary critics have been contending that the production of crude alcohol (a mixture of methylic, ethylic, propylic and buthylic alcohols) to be used as automotive fuel makes no sense energetically. According to them just the distillation process absorbs more energy than is contained in the crude alcohol produced. This is not literally true in the first place. Distillation, though, is certainly the most energy consuming step in the whole process — and it can be carried out without burning a single drop of oil, using solar energy. The returns on invested capital are much higher when solar energy is used to distill alcohol, than when it is used to distill water in desalination plants.

Again the production of alcohol from agricultural waste — as well as all other types of generation of energy from biomass — could not solve by itself the energy crisis. There can be no single solution, no individual intervention decisive enough to put everything right in the energy field. Many innovations, many interventions will have to be designed and implemented simultaneously. They will have to be negotiated and coordinated by the various groups of people and by the various governments involved.

Some experts tend to ridicule the contribution that can be given by solar, wind and biomass energy. They point out that all three sources together would provide, at most, 15% of the total primary energy needed by an industrial nation. This may well be true. Note, however, that — in case the flow of oil from the Middle East were to stop suddenly — for most European nations and for Japan, having this extra 15% would mean disposing of half as much energy as they would otherwise be left with.

So we should work hard at all types of alternative energy sources. However, alternative energy strategies are at least as important. Among these, conservation strategies are the most important, because roughly half of the primary energy generated in any industrial nation ends up being wasted. Very roughly and approximately: 10% is lost in the transportation sector, 10% is lost in industrial uses, 10% is lost in domestic and commercial uses and 20% represents losses incurred in the generation of electric energy. Since the latter is the largest single item, it is appropriate that we analyze it more closely.

Hydroelectric power stations are well known to be very efficient. Only a few per cent of energy potentially stored in the water is lost in the process of generation. Losses are very high in thermoelectric power stations, whether exploiting the combustion heat of mineral fuels or the heat produced in a fission nuclear reactor. The efficiency of a thermoelectric power station can go from 26% (for gas turbines) to 40% (for steam turbines). This means that between 60% and 74% of the thermal energy produced is lost, with no benefit for anybody and possibly with negative effects on the environment. The advantages to be obtained if that lost energy were to be recuperated would be remarkable indeed. The fact that so much thermal energy has to be dissipated any time that heat is transformed in mechanical energy, is unavoidable because of the second principle of thermodynamics. There is no physical principle, though, which states that the dissipated heat should be thrown away.

The problem here is that the total quantities of heat to be dissipated at a relatively low temperature are quite huge and that large users of heat are not always conveniently located in the vicinity of thermoelectric power stations.

The best way of utilizing this dissipated heat, which otherwise would be lost, is to use it for heating space and water for domestic, commercial and business users in whole urban areas. The power stations are then attributed the functions of generating heat as well as electricity and they are called co-generation plants. The low temperature heat from the co-generation plants is transmitted to the urban districts to be served by means of large insulated water pipes, which have diameters up to one meter and which form distribution networks of many dozen kilometers. The heat from this primary network is transferred to the users by means of heat exchangers. The return pipes from the primary network to the co-generation plant in certain Swedish cities (e.g. in Västerås) pass under the mains streets and are not thermically insulated. Consequently in winter they thaw the snow automatically and avoid the need for snowploughs.

Naturally district heating and co-generation plants find their typical use in Northern countries and in winter. This technology has been applied since the early Twenties in the Scandinavian countries and since the Thirties in the Soviet Union. More recently co-generation plants have been installed in Germany (Saarbrucken), in Canada and in Northern Italy (Brescia, Verona).

Public utilities who run co-generation plants normally sell both electricity and heat. In some cases a flat constant tariff is paid for heat, in other cases simple heat meters are used.

The global advantage for the community is obvious. No extra quantities of gasoil or natural gas are used for heating water and space — which improves the balance of payments abroad and decreases pollution levels. The advantage is even greater when the district heating replaces electric heating. Even in countries like Sweden or Norway, where hydroelectric power is abundant, the elimination of electric heating permits to minimize the electricity produced by thermoelectric plants and to avoid one of the most wasteful and unnatural arrangements for using energy. In fact, as we have seen, when a thermo-electric power station transforms heat into electricity, about two thirds of the energy is lost in the process. Electric power is much more useful and flexible than thermal power: it can be easily transmitted over long distances, it can be transformed back into mechanical power, it can feed electronic equipment, it can provide light. Consequently the low transformation efficiency is well justified. It is not justified any longer, though, if the electric power is transformed back into heat. Then the waste of two thirds of the original energy is too stiff a price to pay for the comfort and cleanliness of the final user.

Co-generation plants which provide also district heating have a global efficiency of 60 to 70%. This is much higher than the 25 to 40% efficiency of thermoelectric power stations, in which the relatively low temperature ($150-250°C$) heat is just dissipated in the air or in the water of a river, lake, or the sea. However, a considerable portion of the available heat is lost on the way from the power station to the urban district that receives the heat. More heat is lost, of course, the longer the distance from power station to urban area. Less heat is lost, when the large pipes carrying warm water are better insulated. On the other hand, better insulation and longer transmission distance make for a more expensive installation and a higher investment.

Co-generation and district heating systems (also called total energy systems) may be installed a lot more cheaply if they are designed into the project of a new urban district from the beginning. If they have to be inserted into an existing urban structure, retrofitting problems are quite serious and the system is much more expensive.

The situation would be much more favorable with much smaller co-generation plants. The heat could then be produced quite near to the users and even within individual homes. Heat losses and retrofitting expenses would both be minimized.

The small co-generation plants would replace many gas or gasoil boilers used for heating space, which also have quite low efficiencies of about 60 to 65%. The reason why these efficiencies are so low has nothing to do with the second principle of thermodynamics. The reason is that the gas or gasoil flames have very high temperatures (about 2,000°C): to extract all the produced heat (that is to bring down the temperature of smoke at the stack to about 100°C) it would be necessary to install heat exchangers which would have to be too large and expensive.

A solution just of this type has been found by Cummins Engine, who are installing in downtown New York diesel engines, each of which generates a few hundred kilowatts and, at the same time, provides heat for the space of many flats and offices. Some critics (among which Consolidated Edison, who lose business when their customers stop buying electricity and heat from them and generate their own) maintain that these large diesel installations add too much pollution to downtown areas.

Fiat in Italy has offered a less polluting solution, based on small total energy modules, which use a small 900 cc car engine running on methane. The engine drives an asynchronous generator which synchronizes automatically on the network and which produces 16 kilowatts. The heat obtained from the radiator, from the exhaust gases (much cleaner than a diesel exhaust), from the oil and from the water cooled electric generator, is transmitted to water which circulates in normal radiators and can heat four small 100 square meter flats.

The 16 kilowatts generated by the Fiat module represent, again, only one fourth of the total potential power released by the methane. The efficiency of this type of electricity generation is still 25%. The remaining 75% of the energy produced, though, is used on the spot, so it does not have to go through long pipes. Consequently the efficiency with which this dissipated energy can be used is about 87%, which means that 90% of the energy potentially contained in the natural gas can be actually exploited.

The price of a TOTEM (as these Total Energy Modules have been called commercially) is about three times as high as the price of an equivalent traditional boiler. A TOTEM operates only during the cold season and it may run for about 2,000 hours per year. In a year it generates 32,000 kilowatt hours, the selling price of which is of the same order of magnitude as the difference in price between the TOTEM and the traditional boiler. This means that these small total energy modules can be amortized quickly. How quickly depends on the actual prices of electric energy, gasoil and natural gas. In fact it would be reasonable to sell natural gas at a lower price to users who generate with it both electricity and heat, rather than burn it for heat alone. But this would be only one instance among the very many reasonable ones of designing price structures so that the public gets an incentive to make choices which are beneficial to the whole community.

There is no doubt that a large diffusion of small total energy modules would be beneficial to any community in countries where winters are cold enough to require space heating.

Suppose that in a given country 170,000 TOTEMs are installed and that on the average they operate for 2,000 hours per year. At 16 kilowatts each, these units would produce in a year 5.44 TWh (1 TWh or terawatt hour equals one billion kilowatt hours or 10^9 kilowatt hours). With the efficiency of about 33% of a thermoelectric power station, this energy would require about 9 million barrels of oil to be produced, which — at $20 per barrel — would cost $180 million. The saving is remarkable, both in terms of money and in terms of barrels of oil.

It is even more remarkable, though, that the energy produced in a year by those 170,000 TOTEMs is the same as the energy produced in one year by a 1,000 MW nuclear power station. That is supposing that — barring incidents, sabotage and demonstrations of anti-nuclear movements — the nuclear power station operates for 5,500 hours a year.

So one big nuclear power station and 170,000 small total energy modules produce in a year the same quantity of electricity. Between the two solutions there are also the following differences:

- the cost of a 1,000 MW nuclear power station is about one billion dollars: the cost of the 170,000 TOTEMs is just about half a billion dollars;
- the efficiency of most nuclear power stations (which do not have co-generation capabilities) is about 40% — the efficiency of the TOTEMs is about 90%;
- the calendar time necessary for building a nuclear power station is about ten years — or more, if the antinuclear movements oppose it with particular strength: the time necessary for building and installing 170,000 TOTEMs is less than one year.

A large scale diffusion of small total energy modules would then decrease our dependence on oil. Over the short and the medium term it could represent a very important contribution to the solution of the energy crisis — until, hopefully, long term strategies will become operational.

A snag of the small total energy modules is that users switch them on when they need heat. From that moment they also begin to pour on the electric network 16 kW of electric power, irrespective whether there is demand for it or not. When too many users need heat at a time when the network does not require electricity, we have the problem of storing the extra power produced. The simplest way to store large amounts of energy is to pump water back into hydroelectric reservoirs, pushing up their levels. Later, when there is a peak of electricity demand, that same water is made to flow back through the turbines. The efficiency of the whole process is about 75%, not too stiff a price to pay for transforming off-peak low value energy into peak hour energy.

A second snag, of course, is that methane or natural gas may also become unavailable. One of the advantages of using natural gas in Europe is that — at least — its suppliers are not the same parties who supply oil. Natural gas, in fact, comes from Algeria and Russia — whereas oil comes from the Persian Gulf and Libya. Some help may come from biogas — or methane produced from the digestion of organic waste, urban or agricultural. In China, about two million small installations have been made in the Szechwan region for the production of methane from cattle manure. A modern dairy with 60 head of cattle can produce about 12,000 m³ of methane a year. This is sufficient for 2,000 hours operation of a TOTEM module, producing 16 kW of electricity and heating at the same time about 1,200 m³ of space (homes, or possibly hothouses).

Total energy modules running on natural gas cannot be used to advantage during summer or in warmer climates. We could get around this difficulty analyzing accurately what kind of industrial processes can benefit from low temperature heat. In some areas near the ocean, the low temperature heat can be used together with solar heat for desalting sea water. In other areas the low temperature heat can be used — again in conjunction with solar energy — to distill alcohol from fermented liquids derived from sawdust, straw and other vegetable waste.

I have not even mentioned in this chapter the well known major sources of energy, some of which could be argued to represent alone a general solution to the energy predicament. These are:

- coal, available in very large amounts in Northern Europe, England and America. The snag here, is that it causes excessive pollution. Another snag is that it is unequally distributed
- oil shale, available in large amounts in North America. Although an economic and proven process for the extraction of oil has not been found yet
- geothermal energy, which has limited availability. The prospects of geothermal energy in the United States have been bogged down in red tape even after 1973
- nuclear fusion — a phenomenon which takes place in hydrogen bombs, but which no one has yet proven in controlled conditions. Nuclear fusion power stations will probably be available only during the next century
- hydroelectric power: a strong case in favor of it is presented in the next chapter (p. 98 ff.).

The point I wanted to make is that there are no magical solutions and that some modest alternatives can bring contributions which are more important than people commonly believe.

The energy crisis will be solved only with systemic conjunctions of many different innovations, rationalizations and interventions. Small and large solutions will have to be accepted: each at the right time and in the right place.

CHAPTER 8

Reasonable Arguments and Lists Reasoned Out

THE *International Development Review* publishes a quarterly supplement called *Focus* which publishes articles on the theory and practice of international activities of technological cooperation and assistance. In the third issue of 1976, Dennis Schroeder quotes a number of arguments of the Nigerian economist Ademola Banjo against intermediate technology in general. The more interesting of these arguments are:

— "If people must learn new technologies, they might as well learn the most modern and effective ones since the intellectual effort is much the same
— The cost of a particular plant installation with older technology might be lower, but because of lower productivity, the actual cost per unit produced may be higher
— Increased employment can only be obtained with increased productivity, which would lower costs and promote consumption and the ability to compete in export markets."

The first of these three statements is the most debatable. It is reasonable to think that technologies and machines which require smaller investments are simpler than those which require higher investment and that we can learn simple technologies more easily than complex ones. A serious discussion on the subject, though, cannot proceed simply from general principles nor from what appears to be reasonable to some participants in the debate. It is more appropriate to decide case by case, taking into account all relevant elements: what the technologies are from which we can choose, in which society they have to be applied and for what purpose.

The second and third statements by Banjo are acceptable as long as they are not used to beg the question of the goals to be achieved with the introduction of new technology and as long as they are not considered as absolutely and generally valid.

We should not always pursue the goal of minimizing the cost of every product to the exclusion of any other goal. We can imagine situations in which we can accept to produce some new object at a higher cost, counterbalancing this disadvantage over the long term with other advantages — like the technical training of a larger number of persons. The products of a new technology are not always meant to be exported: when they are aimed at the domestic market, the third statement loses part of its validity.

In the same article Schroeder wonders whether "perhaps the argument is not so much over what the technology should be as who decides what it should be". This question would not be so relevant were it not for the fact that people in general prefer to have their own way, rather than follow the orders or the authoritative advice of someone else. We can try, then, to express a similar concept: in other words a new technology which entails higher production costs and worse operating conditions than another, all considered, may be preferred to the alternative, if the persons involved (decision makers, operators, final users) accept it with so much enthusiasm that their own more effective contribution compensates the other factually adverse factors.

The field of modest or intermediate technologies is not very well defined. We should consider and define more clearly many solutions which can be imagined, which are superficially similar one to the other, but which present also marked differences. We cannot hope to single out a small set of guiding principles to be used for solving all the dilemmas we meet on our way. We probably will not be able to demand formal proof of the coherence of all proposals, but we should at least discard unreasonable general arguments.

The criteria of coherence and reasonability to be applied to possible modest technology projects are similar to those normally used in any other techno-economic endeavor. It may be useful to look at a few of them.

Any innovative enterprise requires a certain quantity of preliminary theoretical studies and analyses. It also requires that some experiments be carried out. These may be constituted by the construction and operation of pilot plants, for example. It is difficult to decide how the available resources should be allotted to these two types of activity: study and practical experimentation. The decision is difficult to make in particular instances and it is even more difficult – or impossible – to make in general.

We can safely affirm, though, that any enterprise in the preliminary phase of which only studies are carried out – with no experiments or, on the contrary, only experiments are carried out – with no analysis of data and no theoretical effort, is out of balance and runs serious risks of failure. This statement may sound trivial to you, if you have never come across pragmatism nuts who just carry out experiments without having any idea of what they want to prove or disprove. But these nuts exist. There are also numerous representatives of the opposite extreme position which consists of cranking out innumerable budget forecasts, feasibility studies, research programs without ever comparing them with the real world or reaching any practical decision.

Similar considerations can be made concerning the balance between the efforts devoted to evaluate quantitatively and qualitatively the results reached and the state of completion of work in process, and the efforts which tend to produce new results. The evaluation of what has already been accomplished – in absolute terms and in terms of percent completion – is necessary, but it is easy to slip and to devote excessive attention to it.

In a different field, it is necessary to reach a balance between the resources invested in training new personnel, in order to enable them to take care of sophisticated tasks, and those devoted to an extreme simplification of every technological or production task, so that even untrained personnel may be used productively at once. The latter solution may require excessive expenditures in the activities of production and organization specialists and has the snag that it does not raise the cultural and operational level of employees much. The former solution may be more advantageous over the long term, because it does improve the performance and the employability of personnel, but may require too long before the first trainees are made available for production work.

Professor Emanuele Tosco of Fiat has presented some interesting criteria concerning the introduction of modest technologies in the automotive field, in his paper "Applied Research on Adapted Technologies in the Mechanical Sector and Their Transfer", presented at the International Study Meeting on the Problems of Emerging Africa, held in Rimini in September 1976..

Professor Tosco says that in the mechanical sector modest technologies are relevant as regards production processes and organization aspects: they are not relevant as regards the products proper. In order for the second part of this statement to be correct, we must agree to define the mechanical sector as coinciding with the production in series of fairly complex machines (tractors, small trucks). Artisan-like production, or the production of much smaller units — for which the definition of the products is very relevant indeed — should be excluded from the context of the Tosco arguments, then.

The objectives of this research were to transfer certain production technologies in the mechanical sector to third world countries, keeping unchanged unit costs and quality and:

- keeping down as much as possible production volumes, due to the fact that markets are small
- using as much as possible local cheap labor in order to decrease unemployment and to produce a positive socio-economic impact

— decreasing the ratio between invested capital and total product, because in third world countries available investment capital is well known to be scarce.

A way which favors the achievement of all the above three goals is to abolish all automation intended to decrease the need for manual labor. Automation devices and systems, which are intended to decrease physical exertion of workers and to increase safety, must not be discarded.

The most satisfactory success has been recorded in the production of small intermittent, but repetitive, series of equipment (every series, e.g. of small tractors consisting of machines of exactly the same model as previous series). The production of intermittent and non repetitive series (as in the case of machine tools) or of mass production in a continuous flow (automobiles, appliances) has been less successful.

We must be careful not to trust too much arguments which sound reasonable, but are too vague. Vague statements may be just useless, or — worse still — they may lead to accept opinions which sound plausible and are instead utterly false.

Let me introduce a couple of examples to illustrate this point. We hear often the statement that new appropriate technology should have a human face. This sounds like a good principle. It should be better for just about any activity to be human rather than inhuman. On the other hand this criterion is misleading because it is too dependent on individual gut feeling and, then, it is next to useless. If we establish a stern quality control department in a plant — irrespectiye whether it is engaged in advanced high technology production or in modest technology manufacturing — this may cause production workers to worry and even to develop a stress syndrome. One might be tempted to conclude that industrial plants which have a stern quality control department are inhuman. A way in which industry would be given a human face, could be to abolish all quality control departments or to make them lax and bland. We know full well, however, that quality is downgraded fast when there is no control. Low quality may be the reason why the market refuses goods manufactured by plants without quality control, which — unless they get subsidies they do not deserve — could then be forced out of business, transforming the production workers into unemployed workers. At that point we would decide that unemployment is more inhuman than work carried out under serious and stern control.

Rather than discuss whether technology has a more or less human face, it will be better to talk about advantages and disadvantages involved by the various possible solutions, trying to determine also who is going to enjoy the advantages or suffer from the disadvantages and when.

The second example concerns the introduction of new technologies in less developed countries. Another current argument contends that we should evaluate any effect that each new technology to be transferred can have on the social life and the culture of the population that is expected to adopt it. This evaluation should confirm that after the projected technology transfer culture and social life will be as valid, interesting and complete as they were before. There are two objections against this argument. The first is that the evaluation of socio-cultural effects of a technology transfer is certainly desirable — but it is also certainly very hard to formulate, so that at best it can only be hypothetical. In other words: it is good to try and foresee the socio-cultural consequences of industrial and technological ventures, but we should not live under the delusion that it is always possible.

The second objection is that we cannot consider as optimized by definition the socio-cultural conditions existing in a less developed country prior to the introduction of new technologies. We may say that they represented a stable situation — provided they had not been changed for a long time, but we cannot maintain they must necessarily have been such to guarantee a good quality of life nor to realize ideal justice and general satisfaction. Quite often, in fact, the contrary is true.

It is better, then, not to idealize the things we deal with nor the abstract concepts we talk about. Let us proceed, rather, to examine a sequence of concrete technological applications.

We have seen in Chapter 7 that in the energy field there are modest solutions consisting in the use of small total energy modules or in the adoption of alternative, renewable energy sources. There are, however, other important enterprises which could be started in the energy field with considerable advantage for all concerned.

It is a commonly accepted fact that in advanced countries practically all technically feasible hydroelectric plants already have been exploited. It is not literally so: the potential yet to be exploited — even if less advantageously than in existing plants — is very high. The percentage of the technically feasible hydroelectric plants[1] actually exploited is 64.4 for Japan, 58.1 for the European Economic Community, 39.2 for the United States and only 6.8 for Comecon countries and U.S.S.R. If we look at continents globally, we have:

	Feasible hydroelectric power plants actually exploited (%)
Europe	41.3
Asia	4.5
Africa	1.7
America	18.9
Oceania	30.5
World	11.8%

From the above table we see that all over the world, but especially in Africa, Asia and America, there is yet a lot of hydroelectric power to be generated: the equivalent of about 1,500 power stations, each with a power of 1,000 MW. The equivalent of 150 such power stations could be installed in Europe, 700 in Asia, 250 in Africa and 400 in America. It would be very advantageous, then, to organize international consortiums and industrial cooperations in order to build these power stations. The power produced would be used for local

---

[1] These and the following data and arguments are taken from: Angelini, A. M., "Utilization of Hydraulic Resources Still Available in the World"; 9th World Energy Conference, Detroit, September 1974.

energy needs and then to process locally ores and other natural resources available on the spot and possibly to produce liquid hydrogen to be transported to advanced countries and used as a non polluting fuel. (Similar proposals — on a larger scale and with much higher risks — have been made for producing liquid hydrogen in nuclear power stations installed on atolls in the Pacific Ocean.)

It is also possible, though, to design and install small water turbines for small flows of water, which would hardly be used in industrialized countries, but which could improve dramatically local energy situations in less developed countries. In these cases, advanced technologies would not be exported nor transferred, but exploited as described to permit other technologies to be used.

This is only an example of a wider class of cases in which advanced industry — with its expensive tools and facilities, with its skilled workers, which can supply low priced, high precision mass productions — can supply tools or machines which make possible the establishment of modest technologies in less developed countries. The most interesting products of advanced countries to be used for the creation of industries based on intermediate technologies in the third world are:

- high quality tools (stainless steel, special alloys, etc.) to be used manually — especially where manual work has now a low efficiency due to the low quality of the tools — or with power supplied by animals for ploughing, lifting water and carrying out other agricultural operations
- bicycles and their parts, used for transporting people and goods (very efficiently, as proved by Vietcong transportation system) and also for producing energy and for driving small machine tools used in agriculture and industry. Professor Stuart Wilson of Oxford University has made a deep study of bicycle technology and he has built many machines, which can be manufactured by advanced industry, as well as by intermediate industry in the third world. For example: hydraulic pumps, pedal lathes,

rickshaws (or vans in which a single man pedals for transporting other persons or goods) with a differential on the rear axle so that speed and safety in turns and bends are considerably increased, grinders, and other machines for processing farm products
— mechanical and electrical components. In an underdeveloped country the first jobs that can be done are wood carpentry (possibly using only hand tools) and metal carpentry (using electric and oxy-acetylene welders and small machine tools). Once adequate plans and designs are available, it is possible to manufacture in third world countries: chassis, bodies, containers and other unrefined components. It would not be as easy to produce ball bearings, bicycle chains, gears — so that these more sophisticated components initially are to be produced in industrialized countries
— structural multi-use elements. At present these elements have not been designed by anybody. There are steel profiles of all sizes and shapes. There are standard bolts and nuts. There are pipes of all diameters and thicknesses, made in all kinds of materials. There are no elements which can be used as containers, or as structural elements to be assembled in order to produce larger and more complex constructions, or as sources of simpler structural elements. The fact that there is a need for these multi-use elements is proved by the infinite uses of the classic oil drums, which have a capacity of 160 liters. They are used, of course, as containers and then as burners, kitchens and stoves, floats for rafts, reactors for chemical reactions, rudimentary boilers, filters, Savonius vertical axis windmills (obtained by cutting the drum on a plane which contains its axis and soldering to the vertical axis of rotation the two edges of the cutting which were diametrically opposed before the cut), reservoirs for the production and the storage of biogas, mixers, and so on. Since the oil drums have found so many uses, which certainly had not been foreseen by the people who initially designed

them, even more general and crafty use could be found by
an element built along the following specifications:
(1) it should have as its initial function the packaging
of fluids (chemical, food), which need to be shipped in
vessels and then to be distributed in modest quantities
(2) it should be smaller than an oil drum: a capacity of
about 20 liters appears to be reasonable, so the element
is easy to handle when full and apt to be employed in
many ways afterwards
(3) it should not require mechanical rework; in particular
it should be easy to make additional holes in its walls
so it can be mounted together with other identical elements
by means of nuts and bolts. The holes can be foreseen by
means of punchouts, or circular areas on the walls on
which the thickness has been reduced; it should also be possible to separate the element in component parts in more
ways than one, according to the various possible re-uses
(4) it should be built with an alloy that can be easily
brazed or soldered.

These industrial initiatives conceived in industrialized countries for the benefit and the final use in less developed countries
are typical of the activity of the Intermediate Technology
Development Group (ITDG) established by Schumacher in
England. Stuart Wilson too works in connection with this
group. They are doing a very good job. Perhaps the only thing
I have not found in their literature (which they mail around
free) is the above idea of a multi-use container and structural
element. In case they have not had the idea yet, I would be
pleased if they would take it up and use it.

Schumacher's ITDG has worked out a number of ventures
or activities which can be pursued by new independent businesses in the third world.

A list of the industrial ventures which are described in the
publications of ITDG, may be subdivided in the three sectors
of chemical industry, agriculture and processing of agricultural
products, and manufacturing.

In the chemical industry the more common and easy productions are:

— caustic soda
— sodium carbonate
— sodium hypoclorite
— soap
— tannin, lignin, acetic acid, methanol and other wood derivatives.

In the agricultural sector the most promising activities are:

— irrigation
— threshing and grinding
— ground levelling
— mechanization of cultivation and planting
— sugar factories.

In manufacturing:

— brick works
— production of cement substitutes like lime pozzolana mortars, which can be produced using heat at much lower temperatures than cement
— production of wood and metal window and door frames
— weaving and textile industries
— shoe manufacturing.

Not only production procedures and techniques are important. It is also essential that safe storage facilities for goods which are apt to deteriorate be built and run efficiently. Every year enormous quantities of goods (particularly food) are destroyed by moulds, rodents and pests because of bad storage. In India about 15% of cereal crops are lost every year.

We have seen a number of intermediate technologies which can be transferred from industrialized countries to less developed countries. Let us see now which intermediate or modest technologies could be introduced in industrialized countries.

Why should we introduce in advanced countries technologies characterized by a low capital investment for each new job they provide? Is it not better for advanced countries to proceed on the path of advanced hard technology? Advanced technology, in fact, is capital intensive, but rewards investment with high productivity and, consequently, with high living standards for all the population.

There are two classic answers to these questions. The first is that hard technology often is based on an excessive use of non renewable resources. More modest technologies could, then, improve this aspect of the situation. The second is that advanced, highly productive technology tends to be more and more automated. It requires less labor and can be said to foster unemployment, which in times of recession has very bad socio-economic consequences.

The only industrial countries which have no unemployment are those with a centrally planned economy. The prices paid for the elimination of unemployment are well known: low productivity and low living standards, diseconomies, and ineffi-ciencies due to the imperfections of central planning and a complete lack of civil liberties. In theory, perhaps, central planning and civil liberties should not exclude each other. In practice, they never go together. Rule out central planning and consider that low investment technologies could be used effectively to fight unemployment in advanced countries, because they can create many jobs without requiring too much capital — hard to find during periods of economic crisis.

This line of reasoning, however, is too simplistic. Let us see why.

We perceive unemployment as a problem, when the absolute number of unemployed workers shows a tendency to increase fast. When many industrial workers lose their jobs, this means that industry's production capacity is only partially exploited. Production could be increased and unemployment decreased — with zero investment — simply by putting to work full time the unused production capacity. Modest technologies which promise *low* unit investment, cannot compete, then, with the *zero* unit investment implied by taking up the slack in traditional industry and business. The fact that modest technologies imply low unit investment cannot be considered as a decisive factor.

A more basic problem is represented by the demand for goods — whichever their origin or technology.

Is there any reason why we should think that demand would be high for goods produced with modest technologies and that it would be low for goods produced with advanced technologies?

The first possible reason is that the production costs — and presumably the selling prices — of goods produced with modest technologies could be a lot lower than those of goods produced traditionally. The quality of these modest goods could also be lower: they would find ready acceptance and wide demand in a poor man's market. The asset of modest technology would be simply that it caters for a poor man's market in advanced countries, where a large portion of the population has become poor. This may well happen in the future — for example, if supplies of crude oil were to be cut off overnight — but it has not happened yet.

The second possible reason is that modest technology could produce new objects, which cannot be produced by traditional advanced industrial plants. This possibility appears to be remote. It is difficult to imagine which innovative products could be manufactured at low cost by simple machines, whereas they could not be produced faster with more expensive and sophisticated machinery. This could be the case only for specialty handmade goods. But it is well known that the cost of labor has caused the price of handmade goods to skyrocket. For example, the well known handmade St. Gallen embroideries and laces have priced themselves out of the market. At present in St. Gallen the only embroideries and laces are machine made, whereas — even in Switzerland — the handmade goods of this type are imported from Hong Kong.

Let us put aside these difficulties for a moment and let us assume that the adoption of modest technologies would be beneficial even in advanced industrial countries. In this case the goods manufactured by the modest technologies would have a market. It would have to be expected that traditional hard-technology industry — in a situation of economic crisis — would also compete for that same market demand. The higher productivity, the larger size and the better commercial organization of traditional advanced business would probably give it an edge over the new modest competitors. So the modest technologies could be crowded out of the market soon after having appeared on it.

A way out would be to protect new modest technology ventures giving them a monopoly for manufacturing certain goods or granting them exclusive rights to supply government authorities or public corporation. This type of intervention, however, could not lead to any situation which can be considered as optimal for the community.

Is there no reasonable way in which modest technologies can be introduced in advanced industrial societies — not as curious and rare exceptions, but on a large enough scale?

I think that the only possible way in which this introduction can be made is to assign to modest technologies a task which is situated upstream with respect to advanced technology. This would be the collecting, packaging and transportation of objects and raw materials to be recycled: metals, paper, containers, etc. This type of job is ill adapted to modern industry, as it requires a lot of labor to be used in the field at a slow pace. Many small independent groups would find it easier to carry out a first selection or a first processing step in the recycling of waste, so as to reduce the cost of further transportation and to make the stuff available in large quantity in a small number of collection centers.

It could be argued here that the small modest and independent outfits would be able to collect the material to be recycled more economically and efficiently only if they did not follow the rules normally imposed on industry. They would be underinsured. They would pay their workers less than the minimum standard rate. They would not pay social security, fringe benefits or accident insurance. If the authorities were to overlook this lack of observance of the rules and if this were a precondition to the success of modest technology, we would not have proved anything. Favoring modest technologies by simply permitting whoever adopts them to break the rules and go scot free, would be a very clumsy and risky way of supplying public subsidy.

Some proponents of modest technologies have suggested an entirely different way to avoid competition between hard advanced technology and soft intermediate technology. This could be achieved if all, or most, goods produced with modest technologies were not to be bought and sold — but only bartered. In a sense this new rule would solve the problem. Small production outfits could more easily keep track of the quirks and peculiarities of bartering. Large companies could never hope to — without adding an immense burden to their book-keeping.

On the other hand the bartering solution would impose that all production and commercial ventures be limited to quite a small scale. Why? Because large scale bartering would have to go through a central clearing house. Cumulative supplies would have to be recorded and eventually credit documents would have to be produced granting the right to receive certain goods which for the moment are not available. Now this would be equivalent to the introduction of a new currency, which could be transformed, at certain rates of exchange, in other currencies. This, in turn, would cause goods produced with modest technologies to be in competition with goods produced by large advanced industries on the — more or less — open market.

A barter economy could only exist on a modest scale among individuals. It would represent a parallel economic system, almost completely separated from the pre-existent traditional one.

Francesco Casatello in his book *Robinson '80* (Mondadori, Milan, 1979) has discussed very reasonably the special case of modest non highly mechanized agriculture in industrialized countries. Many people who live in large cities claim to be fed up with crowding, noise, stress, pollution and crime and say they want to go back to the land. The book analyzes the pros and cons faced by city dwellers going back to country life, as well as the economics and the technology of small farms. Casatello concludes that new small farmers cannot hope to sell any significant portion of their crops on the market, against the competition of large, professional, highly mechanized farmers. They can, however, produce varied crops for their own consumption. This does not even mean that they could be completely self sufficient. They would always need a cash income to purchase at least one fifth of their livelihood as well as tools, seeds and other farm implements. The cash income would have to be provided by pensions or salaries, earned by one or more members of the agricultural community. The agricultural crops would allow, however, these new small farmers to achieve a standard of living much higher than they would be able to get in the cities. This is a very plausible example of a parallel economy. Casatello's book gets down to considerable detail concerning practical and accounting aspects of this parallel economy.

There are other uncertainties — apart from those discussed in this chapter — on the feasibility of introducing modest technologies in advanced countries. Some of these uncertainties are caused by economic questions, particularly pertaining to costs and prices. The next chapter is devoted to their discussion.

CHAPTER 9

When Cynics Don't Even Know Prices

"What is a cynic? A man who knows the price of
everything and the value of nothing."

Oscar Wilde

"SERVICES of a housewife never get counted in the Net
National Product. So, if a man marries his housekeeper, the
Net National Product may go down! Or if a wife arranges with
her neighbor for each to clean the other's house in return for
$4,000 a year, then the Net National Product would go up by
$8,000."[1]

Paul Samuelson opens up a stimulating Appendix to Chapter
10 of his *Economics* handbook, just with these apparently
paradoxical considerations.

It is easy to quote many paradoxes and curiosities concerning the gross national product. People often speak of the gross
national product of a country, implying that it is in the common

---

[1] The Net National Product is defined as the sum total of corporate
profits (including taxes and undistributed profits), income of unincorporated
enterprises, interests, rents, wages and salaries, dividends and indirect business taxes. The Net National Product can be defined — equivalently — as the
sum total of consumption, net investments and government expenditures.

If we add depreciation to the Net National Product — and if we also
add the value of total exports and subtract the value of total imports —
we get the Gross National Product (GNP).

There was no real reason for repeating here the above definitions.
They can, however, be useful to the layman, because they are hardly
ever given explicitly — although very often people talk at length of Gross
or Net National Product, without even knowing what these two factors
really mean.

interest to have it go as high as possible. The ratio between the GNP of a country and the number of its citizens is called the *per capita* GNP. If the GNP *per capita* increases, we can say that on average, citizens are becoming richer. It is curious, then, that when there is a traffic jam and thousands of cars stand still with their engine running, using up gasoline — with no advantage for anybody, except oilmen — the GNP goes up just for that reason. More generally, anytime someone produces certain goods and sells them to someone else, who pays for them and then wastes them or destroys them, the GNP goes up and we all appear to be artificially a little richer.

After we have noted this, we could conclude that the GNP may have some meaning just for economists — but is no use for measuring how rich the citizens of a nation are, nor how good is the quality of their life. Samuelson notes, in fact, that these marginal factors (like services or goods produced for one's own consumption, certain wastes, etc.) are very difficult to determine. Consequently any attempt to include them in the GNP would involve a lot of effort on the part of statisticians and ultimately would just add an ill defined new element into the national product value which, at least, has a simple definition. Samuelson concludes that as long as the number of housewives and the basic habits of an entire population do not change very much, the variations of the GNP will be roughly the same, whether these marginal factors are reckoned in or excluded.

In fact the proportion of housewives on the total female population has changed a lot in the last decades — and it is still changing. The amount of jobs and services that people do for themselves is growing too, partly because the number of artisans has gone down and partly because economic difficulties are one of the motivations for doing it yourself. In almost every country a sizable part of the economy is hidden and not even subject to tax: it corresponds to transactions made for cash by individuals and small businesses. This black activity has been estimated to be as high as 10 or 15% of the GNP. We should then try to take into account these and other trends and discrepancies and we should change accordingly the definition of GNP.

Economists have been discussing at length how they could change the rules. The GNP definition could be changed so that it mirrors not only jobs and services we carry out for our own benefit, but also other elements which are difficult to quantify and which may be used to define the quality of life. Among these:

— mobility, intended not only as availability of public or private transportation means, but also as reliability and absence of traffic jams
— cultural atmosphere (libraries, bookshops, shows, performing arts, schools, institutes for advanced study, professional societies, cultural programs on the mass media)
— low level of crime
— availability of green spaces and absence of pollution, etc.

No agreement has been reached so far, though.

It is not so bad that the GNP continues to be defined in the same old way. After all it is useful to have an operational definition, even if it is not the best ever. What is worse is that the GNP is considered as something sacred and very important, which has to grow all the time. The U.S.A. and the U.S.S.R. look carefully at each other's GNP and try to estimate how fast it is growing. They consider that GNP primacy is a question of prestige and so they try to increase their own GNP as fast as they can. In the meanwhile they overlook the fact that GNP may grow also because of waste and they stop keeping tabs on each other only in order to examine the horrible hypothesis that within a few decades Japan will achieve GNP primacy.

Important economic and political decisions are taken in many countries only in order to let the GNP grow. But we have just seen that the GNP does not measure all the important factors in the life of a country. Consequently a more reasonable and complete definition of GNP would have high practical relevance and not only theoretical interest. Even a radical change in the definition of GNP, however, would not guarantee more enlightened socio-economic decisions. These decisions should be taken in such a way that they maximize the welfare of the community — and of individuals.

Vilfredo Pareto suggested a very stringent optimization criterion. An economic situation is optimal if at least one person is better off in that situation than in any other, while all other persons are at least as well off. Again: we decide how well off people are only on the basis of their availability of money and goods. Normally we also suppose that money can be transformed with no impediments nor losses into any good available on the market — at current prices. We know, instead, that impediments and losses are certainly present when we speak of longer term investments. For example, once we have built a bridge, we cannot decide we want a school instead in the sense that it is not feasible to get back and reuse materials and labor from the completed bridge.

Before deciding public investments, it is normal to carry out cost/benefit analyses. The hypothesis is that investment capital is limited and that it can be used to realize only one among a number of alternative construction programs. For each program we try to determine quantitatively the benefits hoped for and the cost. We, then, choose the program for which the ratio cost/benefit is smaller. We all try to do it every day. We try to buy the things that we consider more useful or beneficial to us and we try to pay as little as possible for them. The good father of a family (*paterfamilias*) was expected to behave just in this way by ancient Roman law. He was to maximize the cost/benefit ratio, with no negligence, without running excessive risks and try to forecast the future as best he could.

As soon as we try to quantify benefits, we meet a first order of difficulties. Benefits are subjective and it is difficult to determine how they are perceived by the people belonging to a large group. It is even more difficult to compute averages and to define the intensity with which a given benefit is preferred over other benefits — and by how many people. Then the evaluation of benefits is conditioned by habit and fashion.

We often hear people talking about the need to change life styles. The choice of a new life style entails the acceptance of new criteria for the assessment of benefits and, consequently, to attributing different values to cost/benefit ratios.

If a large portion of the population chooses a new life style, then the demand for a number of goods will decrease, whereas it will increase for other goods. This does not mean only that the quantities of those goods that are required will go up or down. It means that the entire curves expressing demand as a function of price, will be shifted or will change its shape. Consequently for any given price of a certain good, the quantity demanded by the market will be higher (or lower) than it was in a previous situation.

This is nothing new. Life styles have been changing for a long time and consequently, for example, the demand for candles has dropped considerably in all European countries from 1850 to 1950.

The difficulty of evaluating benefits numerically (even when life styles change rapidly) would not prevent us from computing significant cost/benefit ratios — provided, at least, that costs and prices have some real meaning and are not arbitrary.

The well known classical theory states that prices go down, when quantity supplied goes up, and that prices go up more or less proportionally to demand for a given good. Balance is reached where the curve representing price as a function of demand, intersects the curve representing price as a function of supply. At the intersection point, we can read on the diagram the quantity of the good that is exchanged between suppliers and purchasers and the price at which the exchange takes place. When buyers' preferences change, the demand curves for various goods will be shifted up or down on the diagram, roughly parallel to themselves. When external factors limit very drastically the production of a given good, so that only a small quantity of it is available, then the supply curve for that good becomes a vertical straight line (perpendicular to the quantities coordinate axis) and the price of that good increases very steeply.

This is the theory. In the real world things go differently. After the oil crisis of 1973, the market demand for automobiles dropped considerably. According to the theory, we should have expected the price of automobiles to go down. It went up, instead, because at the same time the salaries of industrial workers and the prices of raw materials had also gone up. This is just an example. There is no doubt that the supply and demand mechanisms are more complicated than the one described by the simple classical theory given above. At the same time there are other powerful factors that influence prices, that warp market mechanisms and that inhibit the optimization of any economic situation. There are five main factors of this type.

The first is that many prices are artificially increased by private or state monopolies.

The second factor is that a number of other prices are fixed — even without explicit understandings or cartel agreements — by industries in a given branch, because the corresponding technostructure imposes a high level of prices. This happens for the advanced products of large industries. Only if these products are highly priced is it possible to get adequate margins and to afford sufficient investments in research and development. Only on this basis is it possible to innovate and to guarantee the products against technological obsolescence and competition. Here again the market does not follow natural unrestrained mechanisms, but is obliged to adapt to a set of prices, which appear as costs in the books of the purchasers of those advanced technology products.

The third factor is that some prices are absolutely rigid, since they are forcibly fixed by governments. These are called political prices and normally they are fixed at a low enough level that poorer citizens will not have to limit too drastically their consumption of certain goods — generally foodstuff. In other cases prices are fixed at certain low levels for unfathomable reasons or just following tradition and precedent. A case in point is that of electrical energy pricing (see page 78).

The fourth factor is similar to the third — except that here prices are set by a supranational authority — like the European Economic Community. These international decisions have to be approved by participating national governments. The goal should be the improvement of the general economic situation of a group of countries.

The fifth factor is represented by agreements between worker unions and business, by which industry accepts to increase salaries and tries at once to pass along the burden to its customers by increasing selling prices.

Costs and prices are, then, to a large extent arbitrary. They are fixed at certain levels often by a whim of private groups or of public powers.

Governments may keep high certain prices in order to favor a group of industries considered essential for the economic survival of the nation. Monopolies keep prices high in order to maximize their profits — even when they maintain they would go bankrupt, if they were to accept even a small reduction. We can say that, at best, these price fixing decisions are taken independently from each other. There are, of course, similarities in the way prices are fixed by monopolies and by technostructures. There are also similarities in the price fixing of a government and the price fixing of an international authority.

We could accept as an axiom that these decisions, non coordinated the ones with the others and often devoid of rational justification, cannot lead to an optimized situation — in whichever way we define an optimum. But there is no need to accept axioms without discussion. We can prove that the general conditions obtained when different forces impose all kinds of independent constraints to costs and prices, are quite remote from optimum conditions and can probably be regarded as random.

A well known theorem in mathematical economy states that in order to obtain a Pareto-optimal situation (see p. 112) the prices of all the goods available on the market should be set equal (or at least proportional) to the corresponding marginal costs[1].

---

[1] The marginal cost of a good is the cost that the producer has to pay for producing an additional unit of that good, beyond those already pro-
cont. overleaf

This means that if we fix a given price so that it is 20% higher than the corresponding marginal . cost, then all other prices should also be set 20% higher than their corresponding marginal costs. In this way we can get a Pareto-optimal situation — given that initial constraint on one price.

Another theorem (by Lipsey and Lancaster) states that the best obtainable situation, if the number of constraints imposed to individual prices is greater than 2, can be defined only with great difficulty and is certainly considerably worse than the Pareto-optimum.

Then a situation where most prices (and costs) are set, the ones independently from the others, without any regard for marginal costs and — in general — without even knowing marginal costs, will be very distant from the optimum. In fact there are no simple laws which permit to determine the end results obtained once a set of prices has been chosen arbitrarily: consequently it will be impossible to foresee the end situation obtained, which will appear almost chosen at random. Quite probably this end situation will be sub-pessimized: we cannot be sure that it will be the worse ever, but it certainly will be much much worse than situations obtainable by a wide choice of prices.

Since the cost appearing in any cost/benefit analysis, are functions of the prevailing set of prices, the above considerations prove also that most cost/benefit analyses are just meaningless exercises.

Cost/benefit analyses are also affected by other serious drawbacks. The uncertainties which affect them grow enor-

duced in a given period of time. The marginal cost is the cost for producing one more car, one more bushel of wheat. Up to a given production level the marginal cost is less than the average cost of that good, because fixed expenses exert a strong influence over the average cost. Beyond that production level, the marginal cost is higher than the average cost (and, starting at that production level, it contributes to cause an increase of the average cost). This happens — although fixed expenses may stay constant — because increasing further the production level involves a less economic use of resources (e.g., workers have to be paid extra for overtime or, more generally, the effects of diminishing returns are felt).

mously, when the project is very large, so that the time to complete it is very long. The costs of materials and components necessary to realize a given project will change in time at different rates. Some will grow faster than others. Some may even decrease, while others go up. In general the cost/benefit ratio will change considerably, as a consequence of these variations in the structure of prices and costs.

So a cost/benefit analysis based on a single set of prices cannot be meaningful. It is necessary to prepare many different versions of it, each based on a different mix of future costs. In practice we can only consider a small number of different assumptions concerning future costs. Mishan has noted that, if we consider only 4 different components of the cost of a project to be completed in 4 years and we were to analyze all the possible combinations of three variations for each price in the first year and 4 variations for each price in the three following years, we would have to compute 20 billion different cost structures. Each of these structures would, then, have to be compared to a number of different situations which define the benefits to be obtained. The constraints due to the size of the problem and the tyranny of time available prevent us even from investigating future uncertainties affecting any cost/benefit analysis.

We know that today's prices and costs are to a large extent arbitrary — or random. We note that their future variations are shrouded in uncertainties. We must conclude, then, that a naive faith in cost/benefit analysis can lead us up the path of completely illusory benefits.

We should not trust existing structures of costs and prices to supply data on which to decide which future programs or enterprises are likely to give the most benefit. We should ask, rather, whether a simple modification of that costs and prices structure could not perhaps improve the general socio-economic situation far more than can be hoped from the projected programs or enterprises.

All these arguments apply more cogently to large size projects. It is unfortunate that at present many major industrial

decisions are simply justified with unsupported statements
to the effect that the corresponding programs will provide a
large number of new jobs.

Let us look at a concrete example. Suppose that in a given
country the national energy plan calls for the construction of
20 nuclear power stations, having each the power of 1,000 MW.
The program has to be completed within 10 years. Let us also
suppose that:

- each nuclear power station will operate for 7,000 hours
  per year, so that it will produce 7 TWh per year[1]. Each
  year two power stations are completed, so the energy
  generated increases by 14 TWh per year and, at the end
  of the tenth year the energy generated by the 20 power
  stations will be 140 TWh per year
- the program is intended to double the production of
  electric power of the country, which, then, at the beginning of the decade considered is also of 140 TWh
- during the decade considered the electric energy content
  of the GNP is absolutely constant
- the initial GNP of the country is $150 billion and that it
  grows at the rate of 7% a year — just like the generation
  and consumption of electric power
- it is actually possible to build, install and start up at such
  a fast clip nuclear power stations of this size — with no
  snag and no opposition
- the unit cost of these nuclear power stations is $1 billion,
  so that the total cost of the program is $20 billion. Let us
  suppose, for simplicity, that there is no inflation and that
  prices and costs simply do not change.

A cost/benefit analysis of this energy plan would record
on the numerator the total investment of $20 billion (we
shall not actualize the sums invested in different years). The

---

[1] TWh means terawatt hour. One terawatt hour equals one billion kilowatt
hours, or 10^{12} watt hours.

benefits to be assessed and quantified in order to get the denominator of the cost/benefit ratio are:

- the very progressive increase of the GNP, in that we assume that the increasing generation of electric power is a prerequisite for the increase of the GNP or is a factor capable of stimulating it
- the increased *per capita* availability of electric energy, which is probably a more significant symptom of a higher living standard, than the mere increase of *per capita* GNP
- a lower rate of increase, or a decrease of crude oil imports, with a beneficial effect on the balance of payments and on the rate of exchange of the national currency with respect to foreign currencies
- an increase of the employment level for the construction of the 20 power stations, as well as because of increased business activity in an expanding economy
- finally a negative benefit (that is an external diseconomy) corresponding to the burden of treating and preserving for long times in safe locations the radioactive waste produced by the power stations. We should add to this negative benefit also the health hazards and the risks of damages to property possibly caused by the pollution produced by radioactive waste. The total value of these possible damages (admittedly difficult to evaluate) has to be multiplied by the probability that the damages will actually occur (which is small, but also quite difficult to evaluate).

We can think of a number of different procedures for quantifying these benefits and attributing to them a money value. Let us not get into the complicated details of these procedures, and let us examine − rather − a possible alternative to the program of building all the 20 nuclear power stations.

The GNP rate of growth of 7% we have assumed corresponds to a doubling of the GNP in the 10 years covered by the energy plan. Now, if we managed to let the GNP grow at the same rate, but also to decrease its electric energy content, we could avoid building some of the 20 power stations. If — implausibly — we managed to halve the energy content of the GNP, we could avoid building any new power stations.

How could we go about decreasing the energy content of the GNP?

Some programs and interventions apt to get just this result have been examined in Chapter 7 (co-generation of heat and electricity; exploitation of alternative sources). The real answer, though, can be provided only by the planning of a low energy society. It would be necessary to design each product, each service, each enterprise in such a way that it implies a smaller consumption of electricity. Many products and services would have to be redesigned, based on this criterion. Aluminum artifacts and tools would be replaced with steel or iron equivalents. Electric heating would have to be outlawed and airconditioning would have to be limited to absolutely essential applications (hospitals, computer centers). Dish-washers would have to disappear. Transmission of information would have to replace personal travel, whenever possible.

If we took all these steps — and probably others as well — and we managed at the end of the ten years to achieve a GNP of $300 billion (doubling the initial value), having built only ten 1,000 MW nuclear power stations, then our cost/benefit ratio would be twice as favorable than in the case of the full program with 20 power stations.

In fact the benefits would be the same, whereas the cost of the energy plan would be halved to $10 billion. The situation would be even better, because the external diseconomies caused by the need for disposing of the radioactive waste would also be halved.

The energy-saving plan intended to achieve these brilliant results, would certainly be a major undertaking. We have seen that it would require a number of strict regulations and constraints to be enforced. It would also require the planning of many technical and social innovations.

Can there be a shortcut? A tempting affirmative answer

could be simply: "Yes. Increase the unit price of electric energy."

Intuitively it stands to reason that people waste energy when its price is too low. On the other hand experience has shown in many different countries that if we increase the price of the kilowatt hour, say, by 10% or by 15%, consumption does not decrease by the same amount, but much less — only a few percent. It would appear, then, that there is scarce hope of spurring energy conservation by increasing the price to the final user. In May 1979, some representatives of member governments of the International Energy Agency (see p. 66) expressed the appalling view that we cannot hope to reduce energy use by increasing energy price.

Curiously enough this appalling view is probably right — in the range of prices that energy happens to have in industrial countries. The fact that fractional increases in the price of electrical energy (or also of other energy forms, at that) do not cause consumption to decrease, just proves by how far prices are too low and at the same time points the way to the right solution. The correct solution is, then, to multiply the price of the kilowatt hour by a factor which can go from 2 to 4 or even 5, depending on the present price level.

Some people may object — superficially — that if we increase the price of energy, we force poor people to consume less, whereas we do not affect the consumption of the rich. Price increasing measures should then be avoided because they are unjust. This argument is untenable because it mixes up the question of the distribution of wealth with energy strategies.

A more just distribution of wealth or income is certainly better than a less just distribution. There are well known arguments for — and against — negative income taxes, which should contribute to a more just distribution. The definition of the best way in which to allot wealth and income cannot certainly be given in simple and general terms. In a given country this definition — which will always be debatable — is influenced by the need for accumulation of investment capital, the industrialization level, the productivity of labor and its past history and an entire host of other socio-economic factors. We would be very naive if we tried to override all these considerations and to achieve distributive justice only by keeping low the price of energy. In this way our energy strategy would simply be the fostering of waste — as it is now.

Increasing the price of energy and, particularly, of electricity would begin by limiting waste, and — more important — would offer an attractive remuneration to manufacturers of implements for the exploitation of alternative energy sources. It would also offer the hope of remuneration to people and outfits engaging in the research and development of new energy sources and of innovations which allow to obtain the same results (objects, services) with less energy. Only after these innovations have been successful, the difference between the energy amount traditionally used and the lesser amount needed after the innovation, is perceived as a waste.

All these consequences essentially coincide with the steps I have previously indicated as necessary to decrease the energy content of the GNP. This confirms that, at least in the case of energy, a rationalization of price can produce as many benefits as an ambitious program of technological innovation.

Other critics are well known to oppose increasing the price of electrical energy, because they fear that this would be amplified in other increases of prices and salary and would ultimately unleash a wild inflation. This fear has been voiced explicitly by government spokesmen in countries where salaries are indicized and where the scaling index depends critically on the prices of gasoline and of electricity. I think it is highly probable that the indicization mechanisms are faulty and should be rationalized, rather than leave them unchanged and base policy decisions on their peculiarities.

In order to discuss rationally all the consequences of increasing the price of the kilowatt hour, we should examine to what extent electrical energy costs actually influence total costs incurred by individual and industrial users.

As regards residential use, electricity accounts for the following percentages of total expenditures of families: which already

U.S.A.	2.2%
United Kingdom	2.1%
Italy	1.2%

gives a first indication to the effect that the budgets of families would not be affected directly to a considerable extent by an electricity price increase. Yet residential consumption accounts for about one third of the total consumption of electricity. These are the portions of electric energy which end up being used in the various sectors of the economy:

	U.S.A.	(%)	U.K.
Industry	38		42
Residential	32		37
Government and public	7		6
Transportation	1		1
Agriculture, fishing	2		3
Commercial	20		11
	100		100

Electricity bills account for the following percentages of the producer's price in the industrial branches indicated below (which are those for which this percentage is higher):

	U.S.A.	(%)	U.K.
Ferrous and non ferrous ores and metals	6.6		2.6
Non metallic mineral products	2.9		3.3
Chemical products	7.4		3.5
Electric goods	0.9		1.27
Motor vehicles	0.48		1.65

(The above data for the United Kingdom have been derived from the EUROSTAT U.K. Input/Output Table 1970; for the United States from: "Survey of Current Business", Bureau of Economic Analysis of the U.S. Department of Commerce, Feb. 1979, Vol. 59, No. 2 (data of 1972).)

For other industrial countries the percentages are of the same order, but, in general, somewhat lower.

Now: electricity accounts for a fairly small percentage of the total selling price of industrial goods. Note also that the above data mirror the situation as it was before the 1973 Kippur energy crisis. It appears highly probable that with higher prices of crude oil and — in a much lower proportion, as we have seen — of electricity, industry has begun a conservation drive to eliminate waste of electric energy with its associated costs. If this has not happened, it appears that there is still space for energy saving in industry.

An incidental conclusion that can be also drawn is that it would be desirable to shorten the time lag with which Input/ Output Leontief tables are compiled and made available in industrial countries. At present this lag is of about 6 years.

Input/Output tables describe in detail which industrial sectors absorb which portions of every industrial sector or branch. Their rows and columns are labelled with the names of 44 (or in certain cases 79) different industrial sectors or branches. They can be used, then, to analyze the multiple relationships between economic factors and activities in a given country.

Input/Output tables can be extrapolated towards future years so they can be used as a mathematical model of a nation's economy. How can we explain, then, that even with these advanced planning tools, advanced countries are not in constantly flourishing economic conditions, but are subjected to all kinds of crises?

The answer is that advanced planning tools are not advanced enough. We cannot really define optimum situations towards which to strive and, even if we did, we would not know which procedures and strategies to use in order to achieve them.

Presumably we should try to maximize the following variables:

— proportion of the active population actually employed

— *per capita* gross national product
— *per capita* energy consumption (provided that constraints are set on the consumption of non renewable resources)
— average cultural level of the population
— economic stability
— free time enjoyed by workers (however they employ it?)

We probably cannot achieve in full all these goals and will have to settle for partial achievement at least of some. Before trying to define a satisfactory combination of these partial achievements, we should define an optimum set of prices — which, in turn, is a prerequisite for carrying out significant cost/benefit analyses.

All these problems are typical of Western mixed economies, where governments may establish guidelines, but are not even trying to plan everything from the center.

Is central planning the real solution?

In Eastern countries central planning has eliminated unemployment, but it has not led to prosperity nor to stability. Central planning in itself is not enough. We need much deeper knowledge of the basic systems mechanisms underlying socioeconomic phenomena. We need the lively and active cooperation of populations. We need a new tradition of culture, of moderation, of balance — but more about this new tradition in the last part of Chapter 12, which deals with strategies. These questions of strategies, knowledge, culture and tradition are even more complex, and more important than those of costs and prices and their significance.

Economists know quite well that to a large extent costs and prices are just artificial numbers and that there is nothing transcendental or sacred about them. They know that often we are obliged to make believe costs and prices are different from those actually prevailing in a given country or on international markets — if we want our accounting to be adequate for reaching some desirable goal. These artificial prices are only used for accounting purposes finalized to make sense of just one single venture. They are called accounting prices — or shadow prices.

For example, it may happen that when we buy a certain good or a certain service, we unavoidably produce a diseconomy: cause some damage to ourselves or to third parties. In cases like this, we can attribute to that good or service a shadow price higher than the actual price, as a reminder that the diseconomy has to be paid for: its amount has to be added to the cost.

We can choose shadow prices lower than market prices, when the acquisition of certain goods or services causes additional advantages or external economies possibly enjoyed by third parties.

Shadow prices are often used for certain materials, which a certain country imports and which it charges with very high customs duties. The shadow price of that material, then, is not the price on the international market, nor the price on the internal market after customs duties have been paid: it is, rather, the market price of some other good the country decides not to import, just in order to preserve amounts of foreign currency needed to buy that first material.

Of course there is no guarantee that the customs tariffs imposed by a given country are at all reasonable, nor that the decision to forbid the importation of a certain good and to favor the importation of another, is correct. We use shadow prices just because we realize that actual prices are not significant, are not rational — at least in a certain context. We accept, then, that actual — irrational — prices be used in cost/benefit analysis and so motivate or demotivate individuals and corporations to do or not to do certain things, but we do not accept the same prices as valid for the purpose of public or government planning.

Mishan — in his book *Cost-Benefit Analysis* (p. 83, note) — has written:

> "The economist may, indeed he should, urge on the authorities the need for a change to more 'rational' economic policies. But once he comes to making cost-benefit estimates, they are to be made by reference to those

economic policies that are likely to prevail, not those that 'ought' to prevail."[1]

I disagree with this point of view. Cost/benefit analyses drawn according to all existing rules can only lead to myopic attempts of securing short term advantages. If the rules were the right ones, many of those advantages would be unattainable — and rightly so.

Once we realize that the costs on which we are about to base a cost/benefit analysis are irrational — or random, we should ask ourselves whether rationalizing that state of affairs can provide more benefits than all those our project is meant to bring.

We are a long way from being able to formulate a program of socio-economic rationalization.

As long as we do not have one, we will have to try and be rational, more on the basis of common sense and intuition than of precise calculations. We will have to be wary of ruling out new solutions of socio-economic problems just because a cost/benefit analysis indicates that some old solutions are better. This applies particularly to innovative and possibly paradoxical innovations like modest technological ones.

Meanwhile, certain tools which are necessary for thinking more rationally about problems which have simultaneously social, economic and technological aspects are being made available. These are new analytical and decisional systems procedures — like those proposed by John Warfield and by Hartmut Bossel, which are described in Chapter 14.

[1] Inverted commas are Mishan's — not mine.

CHAPTER 10

The Costs of Risks

JUST after the end of World War Two many Italian roads were heavily damaged and many were interrupted. The big job of reconstruction had not started. Many industrial plants were destroyed. The number of unemployed workers was at an all-time high.

It would have been reasonable and beneficial to steer a small army of unemployed to repairing and rebuilding the roads. It is well known that — sooner or later — this was actually done. There was, however, a brief period in which a well meaning bureaucrat arranged for unemployed workers to carry out *lavori a regìa* — or "work under direction". This consisted of having a team of workers dig a very large hole in the ground on a certain day and — the next day — ordering them to fill it up again.

For the ministry that paid the salaries to the workers *a regìa* the benefit/cost ratio should have been zero. In fact there was no benefit — apart from the meager satisfaction of paying salaries rather than subsidies.

The workers employed in this way had a paid job — as a pro. They also had the con of realizing they were citizens of a country in which such idiotic decisions could be taken.

In this case it would have had no meaning to speak of the risk of doing business for the entrepreneur. The public entrepreneur had decided in advance to choose the worse possible alternative of a guaranteed loss.

Entrepreneurs run risks in mixed economies — unless they cheat or they manage to get (now rare) cost plus contracts, which feature safe built-in margins.

112

The risks of doing business reflect the probability of unforeseen financial losses, possibly of bankruptcy as well as of losing on lawsuits brought by competitors, dissatisfied customers or even suppliers and third parties. Entrepreneurs compensate the fear of risks with their hopes of gain or returns on invested capital.

It is well known that invested capital does not always get returns. Shares do not always get earnings. Industrial and commercial corporations of all sizes go on losing money even for years. On the average, however, every commercial or industrial sector does make money. If we measure net profit before taxes as a percent of billings, it can go on the average from a few percent to even 10 or 20%. This means that the losses of certain corporations are more than offset on the average by the profits of successful companies.

In mixed economy countries, governments oblige entrepreneurs to obey certain rules and constraints — like: minimum wages for different classes of workers, fringe benefits, pension and insurance schemes, safety regulations and so on. It is expensive to follow these rules: entrepreneurs are supposed to get the corresponding costs from their gross margins.

In Chapter 8 (p. 90) I anticipated the argument that too optimistic views on the feasibility of introducing modest technologies could be reached, if simply modest technologists were favored by allowing them to break certain business rules. A similar warning has to be given concerning safety and the prevention of accidents.

This is sensitive ground. Some people will speak of any casualty on the job in industry as of a "white murder". Other people — at the opposite end of the spectrum — tend to ignore the issue, speaking of unavoidable fate and of compliance with existing regulations. The right approach involves, instead, the appreciation and the analysis of risk factors, probabilities, risk perception, safety training, cost of prevention programs and cost of accident insurance.

As in all other fields, it is obviously possible to be over-insured against accidents (life, fire, third party damages, etc.).

If one is overinsured beyond certain limits, the corresponding burden to a commercial or industrial concern can be so high as to cause bankruptcy. This would be an extreme case, but it is offered as a reminder that there is no possibility of totally eliminating risks.

In the old times artisans and individual entrepreneurs would run all the risks of their trade with no insurance whatsoever. When they died on the job this usually meant ruin for their family. We should be careful, then, not to force private entrepreneurs, who intend to introduce modest technologies, to behave like the artisans of the past. Innovative entrepreneurs should not be pushed to prove the soundness of their ideas up to the point of having to pay the price of being underinsured and of running unreasonably high risks.

A simple way to decrease the investment for each new job created is just to save money on safety. One can save a few percent of the cost of a new machine tool if one just omits protective devices (shields, electrical safeguards, etc.). A few more percent can be shaved off the cost by using undersized electric cables. Later, of course, these cables will overheat and reach higher temperatures: the insulation can be damaged by the heat and one can have as a consequence short circuits or electrocutions.

Money can be saved by not grounding motors and other electrical equipment, or using inadequate grounding circuits.

In advanced countries the safety of industrial plants is checked more carefully in the case of larger outfits (bar rare cases of illegality and bribery). Smaller plants and workshops are watched less closely by government inspectors and, in fact, they often work in marginal safety conditions. In less developed countries the situation is much worse.

But let us look at the figures for 12 industrial countries: Denmark, Ireland, United Kingdom, Holland, Belgium, West Germany, France, Italy, Canada, United States, Japan and Australia. According to the UN Demographic Yearbook of 1972, the following table gives the number of deaths for 100,000 population as an average (weighted on the basis of population) of the 12 countries, for three different causes.

	Deaths per 100,000 population Average 12 industrial countries
Motor vehicle accident	23.8
All other accidents	27.9
Suicide	12.7

The table shows that suicides and traffic accidents cause considerably more deaths than all other accidents together (on the job, in the house, in the country, fires, drowning, poisoning, etc.). For the United States the yearly number of industrial casualties on the job is considerably less than the number of casualties due to traffic accidents. On the average for the 12 countries considered, casualties for industrial accidents reach roughly the same number as suicides.

The general situation of safety in industry cannot be said to be disastrous. Some critics contend, though, that official statistics are unreliable and are too optimistic.

When we propose the introduction of modest technologies, we should be careful not to create situations which are much more dangerous than the average industrial conditions. If we do — apart from causing avoidable injuries and deaths — we would contribute to causing the rejection, for the wrong causes, of technologies and production procedures, which could be quite advantageous.

When we talk about risks, safety on the job should not be the only consideration. We should consider pollution risks — but these, almost by definition, should not represent a significant factor in the case of modest technologies.

Goods produced with modest technologies, on the other hand, could cause serious damage to their final users. Let us see why.

In recent years in industrial countries — and particularly in the United States — wide acceptance has been gained by the point of view that each manufacturer is to be held accountable for any damage, drawback, snag, or simply for any excessive and unexpected burden supported by the final user as a consequence of buying and using the manufacturer's products.

Customers — consumers in general — have raised their protests higher — and they have caught the ear of the courts. Many organizations and movements have come up to defend consumers. Some of these outfits have built up a reputation of being monsters of efficiency — like Nader's Raiders.

This situation has induced American — and also European corporations to be much more prudent. New products are now tested extensively to try and determine all possible ways and situations in which they can damage users or third parties.

Many companies — when they realize that a product they have put on the market is faulty and possibly dangerous — warn their customers and recall the product to their plants, so they can modify and improve it. In the United States companies are sometimes ordered by various government agencies to recall certain products.

Of course products are recalled to the factory for modifications only when they have a high enough unit price — so the manufacturer's margin is plausibly expected to cover his accountability. Manufacturers also use recalls as demonstrations of good faith and as occasions for propaganda.

Product accountability has been consistently overlooked by all authors who have dealt with modest technologies. It is, instead, a very important and critical question.

Modest technology manufacturers try to operate as economically as possible. They not only try to minimize initial investment — they also try to keep general and indirect expenses to a minimum. Now indirect expenses have to cover salaries and operating expenditures for:

- safety analysts and experimenters
- designers, in charge of modifications intended to make the products safer
- quality control people
- planners, who decide whether to manufacture or not intrinsically dangerous products.

Now: if all these people are absent or if too few have been put on the payroll or if their salaries are so low that only the worst performers in the profession are hired — then control of the safety features of the products will be minimal and ineffective. In these conditions the risks run by the modest technology entrepreneur will be correspondingly high.

It is not an easy job to assess risks and probable burdens consequent to the attribution of civil or penal responsibilities for real or alleged faults of a product. This assessment is not any easier if the product is a very simple machine.

It is, then, even more difficult to carry out a cost/benefit analysis, where costs are represented by the salaries of designers, safety experts, quality control people and planners — and benefit is a decrease of the probability of having to compensate damages to customers.

It will not be advisable to embark in hypothetic calculations of this kind. It will be better to recur to a healthy pragmatism. In some cases one can prove that a certain modest technology initiative is the only hope of socio-economic salvation for a given human group. There is no choice then and consideration of other risks will be completely forgotten — except for trying, of course, to manufacture products which are as safe as possible compatibly with the experience and the intuition of designers. If you are drowning, you will grab any rope within reach without asking for its strength test certificate.

The safety standards specified for modest technologies should not be stricter than for traditional technologies. If possible, they should not be a lot less strict either. It serves no purpose to state general principles. Product safety and reliability considerations have an entirely different character if you manufacture welded iron railings to be installed in balconies of tall buildings — or if you manufacture commercial envelopes.

There is an important point to be made here. Real risks — as they are anticipated by probability theory and regularly confirmed by statistics — in general are perceived in a completely distorted way. In some cases they are not perceived at all. This discrepancy between real risks and perceived risks may be caused by ignorance or by mental blocks. The first cause is the more frequent. It is easy to confirm it by looking at the figures.

I will try to prove my case quoting statistical data from the United States, which are available in greater detail than for other countries. The corresponding data for other industrial countries are not much different.

We should be entitled to expect that in advanced countries the ignorance at least concerning the three or four major risks of accident, should not be too blatant. It can be proved easily that it is not so — which justifies even more pessimistic expectations for less developed countries, where less data are available and average cultural levels are lower.

Let us take the risks of death in accidents of various types. I maintain that even cultured professional people in advanced countries (with the possible exception of certain actuaries and insurance experts) have only the vaguest notions of how large these risks are and even how they rank. In other words they do not know which risks are higher and which are lower and by how much.

To prove this statement it would be enough to consider that there are people (even fairly cultured) who are afraid of air travel and do not fly, but have no qualms travelling by car for hundreds of miles. Often the same people think that travelling by train is infinitely safer than any other means of transportation. Statistics prove, instead, that over the same distance the risk of automobile travel is about 36 times higher than the risk of air travel. Travelling by train, instead, is slightly safer than travelling by air — of about 35%.

But we can supply a better proof.

Let us assume everybody knows that in industrialized countries the risk of death by accident which ranks first (which is higher) is the one caused by motor vehicles. This is actually so. For example in the United States the probability of death in a traffic accident per person and per year is 27 per 100,000 inhabitants ($27 \cdot 10^{-5}$) (see on page 115 the corresponding average value for 12 industrial countries — which is slightly lower).

Now try and ask a number of professional people of average culture which is the risk of death by accident which ranks second. In other words: which is the type of accident which is less probable than a traffic accident — but is more probable than any other type. You will realize that nobody knows what it is. Probably you are realizing now that you do not know yourself.

This is curious because it is not a complicated type of accident. It is not a risk which has begun to threaten the citizens of advanced countries only after the industrial revolution. It is a very old risk — that humans have always run. It is probably a risk that ranks first in less developed countries.

It is — very simply — the risk of dying because of a fall: from a window, down the stairs, from a cliff, from a ladder, from a chair, down a ravine — or just stumbling.

Once you have this information, you realize that it is obviously plausible. Falling is dangerous, because the force of gravity is strong and we are continuously within its grasp. It is enough that the center of gravity of our body goes out of the perimeter of supporting points, without being directed towards another stable position, for the fall to be inevitable.

I think that these considerations and observations prove my point. We all know fairly little about risks and we should be careful not to draw the wrong conclusions from consideration of non significant data.

Any time that a risk is not any more a mere hypothesis and leads to the death of one or more persons, the occurrence is tragic. Our emotional participation should not lead us to accept wrong arguments.

When the figures we deal with are much larger or much smaller than those we are used to, we fall easily into error.

Just to supply some raw data which can help to get a better perspective of various types of accident (not illness) which can cause death, I give on page 120 the first 15 lines of a table of probabilities. The data refer to the United States and are taken from H. G. Otway, P. D. Paner, and J. Linnerooth — *Social Values in Risk Acceptance,* International Institute for Applied

Systems Analysis, IIASA Research Memorandum, November 1975.

Nobody can live without ever running any risk. At most we can live in ignorance of the risks we are running — but this is a very different thing. This consideration is not an idle one, and is not a fatalistic one. We get from it the teaching that the total elimination of any risk, anywhere, for anybody is an absurd goal. We may well deprecate the existence of accidents on the job, of traffic accidents and of the many different risks we are continuously running. We should not hope to eliminate them all, because we cannot and because any intervention aimed at reaching this chimera would, in turn, generate other risks. It is reasonable, rather, to aim at the rational reduction of all classes of risk — beginning with those that are more lethal and more probable.

The whole problem of the risks of nuclear power should be reassessed on the basis of credible data. These are difficult to collect, since to date the safety records of the hundreds of nuclear power plants in operation has been quite good. The

Type of accident	Probability of death per person per year
Motor vehicle	$27 \quad 10^{-5}$
Falls	$10 \quad 10^{-5}$
Fire and explosion	$4 \quad 10^{-5}$
Drowning	$2.8 \; 10^{-5}$
Poisoning (from solids, liquids, gases and vapours)	$1.9 \; 10^{-5}$
Firearms	$1.3 \; 10^{-5}$
Machinery	$1.0 \; 10^{-5}$
Water transport	$0.8 \; 10^{-5}$
Aircraft	$0.7 \; 10^{-5}$
Inhalation and ingestion of food	$0.7 \; 10^{-5}$
Falling or projected object	$0.7 \; 10^{-5}$
Mechanical suffocation	$0.6 \; 10^{-5}$
Therapeutic medical and surgical procedures	$0.5 \; 10^{-5}$
Railway (except motor vehicle)	$0.5 \; 10^{-5}$
Electric current	$0.5 \; 10^{-5}$

most serious danger is, by general consent, that of radioactive nuclear waste. We should not forget that the large majority of nuclear waste collected, particularly in American and Russian repositories, has been produced for the military programs. The risk of nuclear warfare — possibly unleashed by mistake — is certainly the most deadly we are running now. An interesting possibility would be the disassembling of all nuclear weapons in order to recuperate the fissile materials and to use them for building nuclear power stations. From a first rough evaluation, it appears that about 150 power stations with an installed power of 1,000 MW, could be built: these would be much less dangerous than the A-bombs and H-bombs from which the fissile material is taken.

The conclusion to be drawn, after these slightly paradoxical examples, is that modest technologies cannot be reasonably rejected, just maintaining they are too risky, for the workers and for the users.

We cannot brand anyone who criticizes modest technology as unsafe, stating that he has a vested interest in the continued existence of traditional hard technology. Perhaps he is just wrong. Perhaps — in certain cases — he is quite right. Each argument has to be evaluated for its merit.

CHAPTER 11

It's All A Question of Organization

"A woman is a sometime thing".

THE first line of the "Porgie and Bess" song could be paraphrased into: "A sale is a sometime thing" — which is more literally true. A sale, the closing of a deal, are hard assignments; you just cannot count on them: sometimes you succeed and sometimes you don't no matter what you do — as salesmen and marketing managers frequently tell us.

It is normal that each of us tries to stress how difficult his job is and consequently how extraordinary his merit in tackling it. This would apply to marketing people too — were it not for the fact that it is true, in a sense, that selling a product is more difficult than manufacturing it.

If the production manager of a plant has technical snags and delivery hitches, he has only himself to blame. His job is deterministic: if he is well organized, if he has set up a tight system of controls and can count on good engineering and design offices — then quality is high, costs are low and there can be no undue and unforeseen delays. Of course a production manager too depends on others: on suppliers, on workers, on nature. His dependence, though, is less risky and final than the dependence of a salesman on the whim — as well as on the needs — of customers and also of course on the strategies, actions and resources of competitors.

There are rules for selling successfully — which should be taught in marketing courses. But even if you follow the rules, your marketing activity is inherently risky: the product you sell

122

may be good — and a competitor may come up with a better one. Your product may be the best — but your customer wants it before you can deliver it. Everything may be all right — but your customer goes broke or prefers a competitor for no sane reason or decides to postpone his order until next year.

If we want new initiatives based on the use of modest technologies to be successful, we have to deal with the problem of organizing the sale of their products.

This problem exists as long as there is no superior paternalistic body which buys at rewarding prices all the production of modest technologists. When these bodies exist, they are also expected to cover any operating loss of the outfits they subsidize. Their activity is not relevant to our discussion, though, because it serves the only purpose of creating a fictional world, which is useless for analyzing the structure, the organization and the advantages offered by modest technologies. The situation is similar to the agricultural activities of Louis XVI in the hameau of the park of Versailles — which had nothing in common with those of an experimental farm.

We must not underestimate the problem of sales, then. We notice, instead, that this problem is frequently underestimated also by conventional industrial and commercial organizations. Many people believe that the efforts and the burdens involved in the operation of an efficient commercial organization are much smaller than those required for manufacturing the objects to be marketed. It is easy to understand why. For production, you have to make an initial investment in machine tools, you have fixed expenses for rent or for the amortization of your premises, you have to buy raw materials and semifinished products, you have to pay salaries to production personnel. For marketing, instead, your costs cover things which appear to be intangible: people who travel to reach a customer and just talk, publicity campaigns to whose effects we all believe to be insensitive, and so on.

The truth is that for a large number of products, marketing expenses are of the same order of magnitude of production costs. Of course it is possible to spend much less for marketing.

If you begin to cut down on sales expenses, at first you don't even notice that it hurts you. Only later you will notice the drop in incoming orders and then, if you want to revive the flow of orders so you can replenish your backlog, you have to open branch offices again and man them with bright and well trained salesmen, you have to increase your advertising budget — you have to spend again a lot of money.

Technologically modest industries have here an additional snag, in that they will probably be rather small. A commercial network, as I just said, is expensive and small companies can ill afford a good one. The size of their market is also small, then, and — since markets oscillate — it can go through periods in which demand is so low that very small companies go bankrupt and disappear from the scene.

Why is it that a small company cannot work well with a small market? Because it is not helped by the law of large numbers and runs high risks of having too many orders to ship in one year and next to none the following year. In order to have a number of customers so large that it is stable and reliable for statistical reasons, companies of all dimensions try to get customers all over the territory of their country and possibly also abroad. A foreign clientele offers the added advantage that in different countries the economic situations of prosperity or recession do not always coincide, so that any business which has a slice of the export market can hope to compensate flagging internal demand with strong demand from abroad.

This is essentially the reason why certain biscuits are baked in Edinburgh and then they are transported to London and eaten there, while biscuits baked in London are transported to Edinburgh and eaten there. Schumacher was shocked and disgusted having observed this situation. He wrote with heavy sarcasm that transporting biscuits or any other foodstuff over hundreds of miles appeared to be almost an essential step in the recipe. Biscuits would not be good, if they were not transported over long distances. Irony is easy. It is also easy to say what we should do for avoiding the efforts wasted in transportation in this way. We should have a central body which would not trust the invisible hand steering production and consumption, which would not wait for any balance obtained through market mechanisms — but would decide for the best who should produce what and for whom and where and in which quantity.

The trouble, of course, is that in countries where this central body actually exists, the problem of biscuits and where they are baked or eaten does not arise — because they do not even manage to produce enough wheat to begin with.

Leaving quips aside — a central organization in charge of supporting the marketing efforts of medium and small companies manufacturing products based on modest technologies could have an important information function. It could inform customers about the products which are available and it could exchange information among manufacturers (on materials, procedures, techniques). An advertising campaign for a set of products manufactured with modest technologies should insist on the advantages these products imply for society higher employment, less waste of energy and of non renewable resources and consequently improvement of the general economic situation. The best advertising experts should be enrolled for this campaign, because historically these do-gooding pitches have not been very convincing. Fascist autarchy in Italy was compulsory and left no alternatives. The buying public has few choices available on the markets of countries with a centrally planned economy. Where there is a choice — like in the United States — the "Buy American" campaigns which are periodically waged have not prevented Volkswagen, and other European and Japanese car manufacturers from getting a big chunk of the American market and the same happened in consumer electronics.

Occasionally ministers of EEC countries suddenly realize that the employment situation in their countries would improve if everybody — of course without compulsion, which would be illegal — just bought domestic cars. Their words have no effect as long as the price paid for a foreign car buys better quality and/or service.

In any case there are no speeches of ministers edifying enough, no advertising stunts convincing enough to induce a good part of the public to buy low quality products, if they are not forced to do so. Quality control, then, is a must and not only for the reasons of safety I have already mentioned. Professional societies with no quality control of the papers published in their journals, become ridiculous academes. Universities with no quality control of the professional and scientific level of students, become silly outfits manufacturing worthless diplomas. Industries with no quality control — of product and of performance — lose their customers' confidence and then their market.

Industrial organization experts tell us that quality control can be achieved in different ways. It can be carried out by production people, or by separate and independent departments. Whoever checks whether a product conforms to specifications or not, is not normally able to draw up the specifications too. A case may be made in favor of centralizing the supervision of specifications and of production standards to ensure that they are adequate for safety and economical. We could, then, think in terms of a central body which should help modest technologists in all activities requiring competence and expertise normally found only in larger industries. So this prospective central body or organization could take responsibility for sales support and for specifications and quality control. It could also provide support for documentation and expert advice for administration.

Artisans and small businessmen normally find it difficult to get a good technical documentation from specialized magazines or from the proceedings of professional societies. This is especially true in non-English speaking countries, since a large majority of the world's scientific and technical literature is produced in English or translated into English, whatever its source. If the artisans and small businessmen improved their technical and linguistic skills, they would be able to get most of the information they need on new products, tools and techniques. This, however, would take a long time. Information retrieval centers could provide a good shortcut, but we should take care not to follow a brute-force approach here. These centers should not try to provide to customers the largest possible number of translated items of information: this number would represent a very misleading measure of effectiveness. Since the customers have special needs, the centers should cater to these needs using specialists for understanding what the real problem of each customer is and then for retrieving and transmitting only relevant information. The specialists will then translate the original documents into the language of the customer or they will encode the information so it will be used more readily and effectively. These specialists would not be just Communicators — as in the A-B-C scheme proposed by Schumacher (see page 30): they should have a good technical background and a wide practical experience.

Small companies are often in trouble, because the people who manage them know too little about administration. For example, they do not know the difference between a cash flow, a profit and loss statement and a balance sheet — and they don't even suspect that trial balances exist. No wonder, then, if some managers — technically very skilled — do not even know whether business is good or bad for their outfits and take disastrous financial decisions. The more typical of these decisions are: excessive, or inadequate, investment in machine tools; scarce control over costs and expenses; ineffective control of inventories, which sometimes lack components necessary for keeping production moving, but more often are overstocked, immobilizing capital, which should be used for the normal life of the company and for minimizing bank interests.

We should not believe that administration problems of small businesses can be solved simply by putting at their disposal electronic data processing centers where the accounting data recorded by the firms are cranked out periodically in a computer. These centers would produce documents difficult to be interpreted and certainly no more significant than the data on which they are based. The main functions of support centers for problems of administration and accounting should be the professional training of small entrepreneurs. Only after the customers understand the meaning and the use of basic accounting procedures, will they get advantage from the processing carried out by electronic data processing centers.

At the same time the support centers for administration problems should be able to supply expert advice on organization problems. Technical and organizational decisions are often made easier by the very fact that certain appropriate factors are examined, such as:

- fixed expenses (what are they? how fixed are they? can they be reduced?)
- break-even level of production and sales (comparison between this level and the estimated maximum dimension of the market)
- return on invested capital; profit (or loss) as percentage of sales
- productivity, per employee (comparison with average productivity per employee for the industry)
- costs and burdens for storage and transportation.

Administration support centers should also teach how to understand inflation, how to cope with it and possibly how to exploit it to advantage. At the present time inflation is galloping at high annual rates and consequently is one of the most important factors influencing management decisions and results. The basic concepts are fairly simple — even though many managers continue to be surprised by cost and price increases, and to behave as if they did not know inflation existed. The right accounting procedures can help to forecast and manage reasonably even though costs (of materials and labor) soar, while selling prices sometimes cannot increase as steeply due to government controls or guidelines.

When inflation is high, special attention is to be paid to the real meaning of active and passive bank interest rates.

The basic message of this chapter is that organization problems must always be considered with the utmost attention, whether one uses hard conventional technologies, or modest technologies — whether one operates in advanced countries or in less developed countries.

It would be a grievous error to believe that we can do away with organization considerations and interventions, once we decide to use modest technologies. The reverse is true.

CHAPTER 12

Strategies for the Introduction of Modest Technologies

IN the Spring of 1977 Daniel Bell gave a talk at the cultural center of the United States Information Service in Rome. He touched upon a number of sociological subjects. He explained what he had really meant to say with his book on the end of ideology. He told a couple of funny stories on the predictive abilities of sociologists and of politicians. Then he talked about social innovation, new pacts and covenants that can be introduced in certain societies. He said that we should not be pessimistic: social innovation is possible — new rules, capable of increasing the stability and the chances for survival of society, will be introduced and accepted. Commenting on his previous statements, Bell quoted as a positive example of success in the acceptance of innovative rules, the introduction and the acceptance of traffic lights and of the rules of behavior they impose.

Ironically in the city of Rome there are a number of traffic lights — ill placed and badly designed — which by common consent of the population (drivers, pedestrians and even traffic policemen) are considered as non-existent. They go on displaying their colors, but if a foreigner stops when the color is red, he is egged on by the angry hooting of all the motorists behind him. This is just a curiosity, but it so happens that I have worked for more than a dozen years to design, manufacture, sell, install and maintain electronic systems for the control of traffic lights of a rather special type. The traffic control systems I sold in Italy and in the rest of Europe, operated with variable timing as a function of the volumes and densities of the traffic actually present. They detected how many vehicles were

130

approaching each branch of each intersection and then attributed to each group of vehicles green times which were adequate to have all of them go through the intersection, but no more. In this way it is possible to avoid the losses of time unavoidable with fixed time traffic controls, which go on working always with the same time intervals and are blind to the actual needs of traffic. My traffic actuated — or intelligent — traffic controls avoided traffic jams and waiting queues and allowed motorists to save both time and fuel. They were not even much more expensive than traditional systems. Notwithstanding all these factors which were favorable to their diffusion, these modern control systems have been only marginally accepted in Europe. Many of the modern traffic actuated systems which have been sold and installed have been badly maintained, so their performance was downgraded and they operate now fixed time. Even in the United States, where the traffic actuated traffic controls were invented more than 50 years ago, the majority of traffic controls currently installed are fixed time.

So, in the discussion after Bell's conference, I objected from the floor that his traffic light argument should have inspired in him much less optimism — if he had looked at all the facts. The relevant point here — which I think is proved by my traffic lights example — is that frequently decision makers reject technological innovations which would be very advantageous to the population, even though they present no snags and they are not even extremely complicated. Decisions — or lack of decisions to innovate — of this type justify the suspicion that there is more at work here than just resistance to change and ingrained habits. I think the additional factor is a completely random one. On a larger scale we can almost speak of a biological proliferation of large technological systems — in the sense that they grow without any real planning or design of the growth. Similarly simple innovations or innovative processes succeed or fail in a random fashion — which is not surprising since no one is taking rational decisions concerning these innovations.

Daniel Bell did not think much of my objection — still I

think it is relevant and that it can explain many difficulties which are met when one tries to introduce modest technologies.

In Chapter 6 I håve tried to analyze the reasons why lack of innovation may be the cause of economic crises. Those arguments, however, pertain mainly to the situation as it has developed in industrialized countries. Even for advanced countries that type of reasoning tends to detect general trends, rather than to explain the mechanisms because of which certain innovations are accepted and flourish, while others are rejected.

A number of interesting papers have been collected by Nicolas Jéquier in the book *Appropriate Technology; Problems and Promises,* published by the Development Centre of OECD, the Organization for Economic Cooperation and Development. The papers collected in the book were presented originally at a Symposium on low cost technologies organized in September 1974 by the OECD Development Centre. The first part of the book concerns problems of semantics, of innovation and of information, questions pertaining to the role of universities and the role of new industries, as well as policies for the introduction of appropriate technologies. The second part of the book consists of about twenty case histories of applications, most of which were attempted in third world countries.

The Jéquier book is important, because it collects many significant modest technology experiences, reasonable discussions on them and indications of groups active in the field as well as of references. As it happens to interdisciplinary international groups, a number of papers collected by Jéquier are only recipes for crashing through doors which are already open — in the sense that they only present obvious considerations, which nobody would even think of contradicting. It is not a serious shortcoming: if you want to be thorough, you cannot discriminate too much.

I also consider irrelevant some nominalistic discussions — to be found in Jéquier's book and frequently heard elsewhere — tending to differentiate between true needs (possibly not even perceived yet by the needy) and actual demand for goods, services, innovation. There are only a few things to say on the subject. Certain needs may be satisfied in different manners. We should not take exception if certain people choose to do so in old fashioned ways and refuse new ones which appear reasonable to their proponents. We should not take exception either, if other people choose not to satisfy at all certain needs or, on the contrary, accept new solutions so promptly that we suspect they have been at the receiving end of hard selling publicity campaigns.

In the Jéquier book there are also less obvious considerations which deserve our attention. For example, considerable success may be obtained supporting private informal outfits employing tinkering modest technicians. Instead, larger development organizations of good repute employing only graduate engineers are often bound to fail because they move slowly, they postpone decisions, they obey to false motivations, they fail to understand the real conditions actually met especially in less developed countries.

It is also reasonable that private commercial and industrial companies — larger than outfits owned and run by a single individual — should be encouraged and given adequate credit lines.

I should add to Jéquier's arguments that an essential pre-requisite for the vitality of new business ventures of all dimensions is the adoption of civilized rules concerning commercial competition. Monopolies (public or private) stifle any new initiative and slow down every action. Excessive price cutting competition tends to downgrade quality, to reduce profits and consequently also to reduce the accumulation of capital which would permit further innovation.

The OECD book stresses repeatedly that modest technologies should be conceived for solving the subsistence and survival problems of the poorest portions of the population in the countries for which they are designed. This means often the rural populations. Obviously this consideration has good and just motivations, but it is not very helpful in devising strategies. We could conclude from it that any effort for the introduction of modest technology should be decentralized and organized on a local basis: if not at the village level, at least at the district or regional level. This, however, entails the risk of duplication of efforts and of laboriously reinventing systems or equipment already invented and built elsewhere.

Documentation and information centers are, then, very important — as already indicated in Chapter 11.

At present the majority of centers, which collect and broadcast information useful for introducing and developing modest technologies are to be found at private voluntary organizations or at some government bodies in third world countries: notably in India. The office for science and technology of AID — the American Agency for International Development — has sponsored the development of industrial research mainly in Latin America.[1]

The problem of broadcasting information and data must be considered together with the problem of generating this information and data — that is of the location of research institutes and of the way in which they are run. Jéquier notes

---

[1] In June 1976 AID published a report with the title *Private Voluntary Organizations and Appropriate Technology* in which the following information centers are mentioned:

   Intermediate Technology Development Group Ltd., London
   VITA, Volunteers in Technical Assistance (Mt. Rainier, U.S.A.)
   Brace Research Institute, Ste. Anne de Bellevue, Canada
   Appropriate Technology Cell, New Delhi, India
   Planning Research and Action Division, Lucknow, India
   Appropriate Technology Development Unit, Varanasi, India
   Industrial Development Division, Engineering Experimental Station, Atlanta, U.S.A.
   Division of Microprojects, Eindhoven, The Netherlands
   Appropriate Technology Centre, Islamabad, Pakistan
   Technology Consultancy Centre, University of Kumasi, Ghana
   Agricultural Engineering Dept., International Rice Research Institute, Manila
   Earth Resources Development Research Institute, Washington, D.C.
   Technonet Asia, Singapore
   TOOL, The Netherlands
   Small Industries Development Network, Georgia, U.S.A.
   East West Technology Development Institute, Hawaii
   Intermediate Technology, Menlo Park, Calif., U.S.A.

that in less developed countries the social costs of research and development activities are very high compared to the very low average *per capita* income and that their efficiency is relatively low. The poorest among less developed countries find, then, that lack of money is the largest obstacle to research activities, possibly oriented towards modest technologies.

The richer among developing countries — typically those having oil incomes — normally choose the way of a modern industrial development and then enrol in the corresponding effort all the available scientists, engineers and technicians. These experts are then taken away from any other research and development activity — like those for intermediate or modest technologies. In these countries the situation resembles the one in industrialized countries, where industry and advanced research (and in some cases military research) absorb the majority of people who could be employed in research. This tends to make even more critical and imminent the slowdown of progress in basic science to be expected, due to the mechanisms described by Derek de Solla Price (see p. 30).

It appears, then, that for solving the problems of technological development — modest or sophisticated — it is necessary to use simultaneously:

— the knowledge, the abilities and the technical tradition available in advanced countries
— the financial means of advanced countries and of third world countries who are rich in natural resources
— the enormous potential human resources represented by the more gifted men and women in the third world.

The above list is already a suggestion of the type of international cooperation we should have. One of the elements of it should be a program of cultural exchange, scholarships and fellowships for a large number of young people from the third world. This program should incorporate the best aspects of the Fullbright and UNESCO programs, but should count on a much bigger effort — probably a few dozen times bigger.

We should not have an excessive faith in the success of new technical solutions of any type in providing all the innovation which is needed in less developed countries, in advanced countries and in the industrial and economic organization in every part of the world. Technical innovation is certainly necessary. We must remember, though, that organizational and systemic innovations are at least as important — and they are not easy to single out and define. In Chapter 14 I will try to illustrate the extreme difficulty of solving problems featuring large numbers and an intrinsically complex structure.

Advanced countries too suffer from serious shortcomings of knowledge, training, traditions and culture, which prevent the solution of economic, social and organization problems. Consequently we cannot hope to find in advanced countries — among social scientists, organization experts, technocrats, politicians — readymade solutions which can be transferred to developing countries.

Many important problems simply will have to wait for their solution until experts — much wiser, more knowledgeable and clever than today's — will appear on the scene. It is not likely that this new breed of experts will be formed at random in present day societies — of the East, of the West, of the South — which we should all consider as culturally deprived.

There have been for a long time now societies in which the needs for food, shelter and clothing have been satisfied for the very large majority of the population — at least in the Northern hemisphere. No society ever existed or exists now in which the cultural needs of the large majority of citizens are adequately satisfied. This does not mean that the school systems are inadequate. Certainly schools in general — but for exceptions, which are relatively rare even in the United States — are chronically inadequate to teach what is known about the world, other than to a few percent of the population. All the societies which have existed up to the present time were not designed to make their members wiser or more knowledgeable. Intelligence and culture flourish here and there at random: they are considered as embellishments basically reserved to a chosen few.

Volunteers in Technical Assistance have a yearly budget of less than half a million dollars. The Intermediate Technology Group has a yearly budget of less than £200,000. With these levels of investment it is possible to do some very interesting things — which these two groups certainly do — but you cannot change the world.

In order to change the world we need a cultural revolution made of knowledge (of notions, too) and of understanding (of processes, of mechanisms, of patterns, of regularities). I see no signs of a significant cultural revolution, not even in the United States — where there is a university or college every 200,000 people and where educational programs on radio and TV are more frequent than in other countries. Notwithstanding these assets, the average cultural level of the population in the United States is not dramatically higher than the corresponding level in European countries, in which educational efforts are much weaker. And yet in the States every year more than $200 million are spent for education through the mass media: this sum is of the same order of magnitude as the whole yearly budget of many national radio and television networks in Europe. This means that it would be necessary to invest every year not $200 million, but probably $2 billion or even $20 billion in educational radio and television in order to produce a significant cultural impact. At present, chronic and structural cultural deficiencies are preventing the solution of technological problems and also of social, economic and political problems.

What is the way out? It has never happened that vast cultural innovation movements have involved hundreds of millions of people, so we cannot pretend we have a recipe with which we can produce them. We can, however, try to single out which initiatives can more plausibly bring about the cultural innovation of which there is so much need.

As I said above, I think that a massive recourse to educational radio and television would have a considerable leverage. But, together with radio and television, it is necessary to step up: the printing of books and periodicals, public and private talks, messages transmitted through the cinema and the theatre, the infiltration of cultural elements in political and religious groups and movements.

How did we get to talk about a general cultural revolution to be started all over the planet, from our initial subject of the strategies for the diffusion of modest technologies? The reason is that partial and modest solutions can eliminate almost subreptitiously quite a number of problems, which would stay unsolved if we tried to attack them frontally and generally. But if we tried to extend the partial and modest solutions, if we tried to use them essentially for changing the rules of the game, we would clash against problems of knowledge, of information and of culture — some of which I tried to analyze in the previous chapters.

I have dedicated to this problem of a dramatic upgrading of average cultural levels of entire populations some chapters of a book I published in 1974 called *Handbook for An Improbable Salvation,* but my arguments have been largely ignored. This is not surprising since individual and collective upgrading have always met with strong resistance and have been widely rejected. They are rejected for theoretical reasons by those who think — erroneously — that average human learning capacity is very low. They are rejected by those who just have no inclination towards work or effort. They are rejected by those who have learnt something — a trade, a profession — and do not want any competitors. They are rejected by those who make decisions — or think they are making them — and by those who govern and who go on believing, like Lao Tze said a few thousand years ago, that ignorant populations are easier to be governed than literate and cultured ones.

There is no hope of victory against all these resistances and obstacles, unless we engage in a maximalistic effort, remembering what was said by Giuseppe Mazzini — that, since we must, we can do something.

Of course cultural resistances and obstacles are not the only ones. There are also imposing economic obstacles which tend to limit innovative investments and traditional investments, modest investments and ambitious ones. To the problem of the scarcity of investment capitals I have dedicated the following chapter.

CHAPTER 13

Is There an Investment Crisis?

"IF you have money, you can make even water flow upwards, rather than down."

This old popular Italian saying probably dates back to a time when motor pumps were not so common.

To pump water in elevated reservoirs or lakes is one of the best ways we have for storing energy, as we have seen in Chapter 7 (p. 74). Another typical case in which it is advantageous to pump water up in the mountain lakes is the one in which we use the energy produced by flowing water hydraulic power stations. During off peak hours, the electrical energy they produce is not in great demand — and there is no way of storing it upstream in the rivers that produce it. Then we should modify that old saying:

"If you want to save — you *must* make water flow upwards."

In fact we could also add that, unless you have already saved — that is: unless you have investment capital available — you cannot even exploit the energy of water that flows normally down. This is because hydroelectric systems require considerable investments. This observation should qualify the feasibility of the huge world wide program for the construction of about 1.5 TW hydroelectric power stations described in Chapter 8 (p. 83). That program is certainly feasible : finding the capital to finance it would be a major undertaking.

In 1975, the research departments of the Chase Manhattan Bank and of Exxon estimated that between 1976 and 1985 the investment demand just for machinery and constructions needed for energy generation and conservation, would be

$900 billion. Note, just for comparison and momentarily disregarding inflation, that until 1969 the whole Gross National Product of the United States was less than $900 billion.

Investment in energy generation and conservation is not the only one needed, though. We also need investment for residential and industrial building (for the United States, Chase and Exxon estimate that these will have to be $1,900 billion in the 1976–85 decade). We need investment in other industrial sectors — and they should be of the same order of magnitude as those for energy generation and conservation.

Total U.S. investment needed for the 1976–85 period (including the growing Federal and State deficit spending) should be $4,500 billion. This means that available investment capital should grow on the average during the decade at the rate of 8.7% a year and that — again on the average — investment capital should amount to 20% of the gross national product.

What is the meaning of these huge figures? Do they mean that it will not be possible to round up these enormous sums? Do they mean that consequently the United States will not be able to sustain the yearly growth rates of energy consumption and of the GNP experienced in recent years? Or do they just mean that the task of finding these large capitals is hard but feasible — and so that growth will be adequate and that everything will be for the best in this best of all possible worlds?

It is not easy to give a sensible answer to these questions. We cannot compute the future — but we can at least examine how the experts' opinions have been changing on this subject.

Throughout 1975 the forecasts of American experts were quite gloomy. Arthur F. Burns — then Chairman of the Federal Reserve Board — warned that continuing devaluation. together with an unemployment rate of 8–9% indicated that something was basically wrong with the U.S. economy. At that time the general outlook was rather pessimistic, but the views of investment experts were not unanimous. Some anticipated that the Dow-Jones Index would go below 300. Others saw the Dow-Jones passing the magic 1,000 threshold within two or three years, because business profits would go up, getting to about 10% of the GNP.

None of the very extreme forecasts have been verified. The Dow-Jones has been hovering around the 800 level for a long time. As we have noted in Chapter 5, things are going somewhat better on the unemployment and inflation fronts. Nobody is coming up with much more favorable forecasts, however — probably because no important new positive facts have come up and at the same time no one can claim to have really understood any better how things are really going.

The gang of diehard optimists, led by Herman Kahn, made a big deal out of waving around a list of 25 catastrophes forecast by someone or other, but which had never taken place. The first on the list was the investment crisis. Kahn was not very credible but neither were all other professional forecasters.

In 1977, though, the signs were better, since investments had grown at a rate of 9% in real terms — that is without taking into account the effects of inflation. And yet economists and businessmen have not become very optimistic because investments have not been made with sufficient continuity and their upturn has not been as fast after the 1974—75 recession as it had happened after other recessions since World War Two.

A bad sign is that the average age of industrial plants and machinery in the United States has been increasing. In 1966, the average age was 15½ years — in 1976 it was 17½ years.

Another symptomatic situation that by itself outweighs the positive indications of stepped up investment I have given above, is the total amount of indebtness. There are signs that Western economies are getting too deep in debt in all sectors — which certainly may put in jeopardy future investments, apart from fueling inflation. This is particularly true of the economy of the United States, where the total debt has been higher than the Gross National Product since 1971. At the end of 1978 the total U.S. debt was of $3,900 billion, subdivided as shown in the table on page 143.

Almost one third of the total debt in the United States was generated in the public sector. In other countries the

Borrower	Debt in billion $
Treasury	700
Federal Agencies	200
State and local government	300
Corporate	1,050
Consumers	300
Mortgage	1,150
Other	200
Total	3,900

Source: *Business Week*, Oct. 16, 1978, p. 76.

situation is even worse. Future deficits will soar also because of the heavy commitments for social security and pension schemes. The indicization of pensions is, of course, a very equitable provision, but if the corresponding mechanism has not been designed with future balance in mind, it can lead to public bankruptcy.

An economy in which the government generates debt rather than money will not have a lot of capital available for investment. Decisions on how to dispose of scarce investment capital are critical, particularly when hopes of getting good returns on investment tend to become slimmer.

At present the hopes of future profits are not very high in most fields. The conclusions that are drawn and the decisions that are made by investors are not influenced only by assessments of the probability of future returns. We have, rather, another example of business motivations and decisions depending essentially on the particular accounting procedures adopted to record and mirror economic reality.

In many countries the basic bullish posture of businessmen and entrepreneurs has led many of them to the curious and unexpected decision of dissimulating losses — rather than profits. In the United States, where corporations publish their profit and loss and balance sheet reports in greater detail than in other countries, this syndrome has been particularly visible.

During inflation periods it is easy to give an erroneous

estimate of the value of a company's inventories. These may well represent the major part of the assets of a company. Their variation can affect the profit and loss statement very heavily.

When costs and prices change rapidly — as they do when inflation is rampant — there are three ways in which we can evaluate the cost of sales of a good that comes from inventory and is sold at a certain price. Since the difference between selling price and cost of sales is the company's gross profit, it is clearly important how we choose to compute the cost of sales.

The first procedure consists in attributing to the good we sell the same cost at which it was originally bought or produced, or rather at which we had bought or produced the oldest item identical to the one we sold, that we still have in stock. This procedure is called FIFO, which means "First In — First Out". Since the cost is expressed in older dollars — which are worth more — and the selling price is measured in newer dollars — which are worth less, during inflation periods this procedure tends to overestimate profits.

The second procedure is called LIFO, which means "Last In — First Out". It consists in using the cost of the last item — bought or produced — which has been recorded in inventory. This leads to computing a higher cost because the cost is expressed in dollars that are not so old. Again, during inflation periods, this procedure is somewhat more conservative than the FIFO one, in the sense that it does not overestimate profits so much.

The third procedure — which is the only really correct one — consists in attributing to the goods we sell the cost at which they can be bought or produced now — that is: their replacement cost. Here cost and selling price are expressed in the same dollars and, again when there is inflation, the gross profit computed in this way is minimum.

The U.S. Securities and Exchange Commission admits all three procedures, but imposes on companies to compute with the same procedure their profit for tax purposes and for reporting to shareholders. Since 1977 the Securities and Exchange Commission has asked about one thousand large U.S. corporations to determine and report the replacement cost value of their inventories — although there was no obligation to report these data to shareholders.

The situation is paradoxical. There are companies which adopt the FIFO or the LIFO procedure. Consequently they declare a higher profit on which they pay taxes and they distribute to shareholders a part of their declared profit after taxes. If these companies were to adopt the replacement cost accounting procedure, they would declare much smaller profits or even a loss and they would pay much less — or even no taxes.

Why would any company adopt an accounting procedure which entails paying more taxes than strictly necessary?

Because in this way they present a more rosy picture to their shareholders and to the market in general and they stand better chances of getting more fresh money in the form of investment. If the same company were to use replacement cost accounting — or simply if shareholders knew the result of using this type of accounting — the picture would look much worse and the reported profits would appear fictitious and only due to a high rate of inflation. Consequently fresh investment capital would be more difficult to obtain.

In 1978, U.S. corporate *pre tax* profits were about $200 billion: just about equal to 10% of the GNP, as it had been predicted by some in 1975. However, *after tax* reported profits were $120 billion and, as indicated above, a large portion of them were blown up because of adoption of FIFO or LIFO procedures. Many companies had reported pretend profits just caused by inflation and had been consequently forced to pay dividends which they could not afford. This very fact worsened their cash situation, which in some cases was the original motivation for reporting artificially improved results. A more realistic figure for after tax profits should have been about $80 billion.

Forecasts on future investments are hard to make — particularly when the very hope of getting returns from the investment is as debatable as we have just seen.

There are other uncertainties, then, apart from those we have already examined in Chapter 9, affecting cost/benefit analyses. There are sound reasons for doubting the profitability and even the solvency of well established traditional companies. Uncertainty is understandably higher for the future profitability of innovative enterprises. In order to define acceptable solutions, it is not enough, then, to establish certain rules for the economic game and to refrain from changing them. It is necessary to make sure that the rules are sensible.

The decision to adopt modest technologies appears to be sensible in the present situation, when it is doubtful that investment capitals available in the future will be adequate. On the other hand the decisions to simplify technologies cannot be simple: they have to be made in a complex environment. To this end it is necessary to employ certain modern techniques which are now available for tackling complexity — as I will try to show in the last chapter.

CHAPTER 14

Decisions for Societal Systems Based on Modern Techniques

WHEN Salvador Allende was killed in September 1973, it was not just a case of reactionary tyrants overthrowing a progressive democratic government. At the same time the junta soldiers also blocked an attempt to apply advanced planning techniques to public policy making. The project was called Cybersin — from the words "cybernetics" and "synergy".

Synergy is the discipline which studies the amplifying effects of actions carried out simultaneously by various people in order to reach certain goals.

I think that the words "cybernetics" and "synergy" are worn out and often carry scarce meaning. Therefore, the name of the Chilean government plan was not the best possible one. But a debate on names is not interesting.

Many experts worked at the Cybersin project. One of the best known was Stafford Beer, the British expert on automatic control systems. Essentially Cybersin was intended to apply systems analysis to the practical running of a government. It should also have optimized the structure, the information flow, the decisions, the plans and the current management of the Chilean nationalized industry. State industry in Chile was subjected to political constraints and to rapid changes — while, of course, it was part of the larger system represented by the country's economy and its social situation.

The Cybersin project only lasted from November 1971 to September 1973. Therefore, it is not possible to assess what kind of results it would have achieved, had it lasted more than two years. We can only argue that the project team did not succeed in producing forecasts and corrective plans adequate to prevent a lethal attack to the government which had initiated it. But, perhaps, this was not one of the assignments of the Cybersin team — and it should have been.

The Cybersin project was described in detail by Hermann Schwember on pages 79–138 of *Concepts and Tools of Computer-assisted Policy Analysis,* a collection of papers edited by Hartmut Bossel (3 volumes published by Birkhäuser, Basel, 1977).

I have cited the Chilean project because its tragic end is an extreme case of strenuous resistance to the introduction of modern procedures in the fields of policy making and planning. Normally innovations are rejected with a more calm, immobile and uncomprehending type of hostility.

The decisions that a government or an international authority have to take in the socio-economic sphere are hard ones in today's world. Ideally decision makers should be competent in a number of different fields at the same time: economics, sociology, law, technology and industry.

The factors and variables belonging to each of these fields interact with factors and variables belonging to many other fields. In order to make decisions that are suitable to reach certain ends, we need not only reliable information concerning all the fields mentioned, but also the help of specialists in the interactions between fields.

There are hardly any specialists of this type today. However, certain modern techniques currently under development tend to create just specialists of this kind. These techniques are establishing procedures, principles and methods which can be used to deal with a complex reality in which large numbers of elements influence each other.

The common feature of all these problems is complexity. There is yet no theory fit to deal with phenomena characterized by considerable complexity or with the ensuing processes and decisions.

We do not even know which conditions are sufficient to handle problems which are complex and which pertain to structures having many interconnected parts. At least we can say that these conditions are not known with any degree of generality. Some conditions necessary for understanding and analyzing complex phenomena, processes and decisions can be at least recognized.

The study of complexity has many aspects and uses many procedures in common with systems engineering. I have tried to describe in simple terms what systems engineering is and how it is used, in the third chapter of my book, *The Coming Dark Age* (Doubleday-Anchor, 1974).

When we consider complex systems and processes, involving very large numbers of people as well as social and human — not just technical — aspects, then certain systems engineering considerations become essential.

Very complex systems structures and processes are rarely suitable for calculations or formal analysis. It is then necessary to carry out informal or intuitive analyses. When these are attempted it is essential that each portion of the work produced by specialists in the design group be continually criticized and revised by other members of the team. Only in this manner we can timely correct conceptual errors and mistaken evaluations made by participants in the study.

The large numbers of people involved in the operation of the technological or socio-economic systems considered, can be operators and/or users. It is essential that all the humans involved — or at least the large majority of them — accept the established rules. In some cases it is also essential that users and operators participate in the definition of the system's structure, so that later misunderstandings and conflicts are avoided.

Participation should include:
- instruction, education and training processes
- recording of preferences or votes in favor of certain solutions as against others
- innovative contributions on the part of a vast population, which has undergone voluntary periods of apprenticeship
- operative cooperation on the part of the general public, based on the previous points.

Instances of this kind of cooperation between government, experts and general public are attempted more and more often in the United States and in other Western countries — but they are not always well conceived so that they often fail.

In countries with centrally planned economies — and with an authoritarian and paternalistic political structure — these cooperations, participations and open discussions are not even attempted. Consequently, since in many cases they appear to be almost mandatory, in this respect Eastern countries are more fragile than Western ones.

It is not only authoritarian governments that inhibit the democratic participation of a wide section of the public. For this participation to exist, experts and specialists have to make an effort in order to explain to the public:

— the basic elements and considerations necessary for understanding what the problem is
— the possible alternatives and policies
— the reasons for which certain alternatives and policies are to be preferred to others.

In some cases these explanations are too difficult and too long. It can also happen that the cost and effort implied by a well integrated program of popularization and explanation outweigh all benefits hoped for as a consequence of the same program. The necessary cancellation of a popularization and participation program may then be wrongly interpreted as the result of an authoritarian action, rather than as the consequence of constraints inherent in the situation.

Jay W. Forrester has claimed that in these fields where complexity is predominant, the correct solutions to problems are often counter-intuitive. At first sight the best solutions seem not even plausible and those which intuitively seem right turn out to be very bad, when subjected to deeper analysis. This view of Forrester certainly should not be taken to mean that all solutions to complex problems must necessarily seem *a priori* unreasonable in order to be correct. It would be more appropriate, then, to speak of non intuitive rather than counter-intuitive explanations. In fact we may say that every time we have to carry out a calculation — either in the course of a technical design activity or of an administrative job — we are following a formal procedure precisely because we would not be able to arrive at the solution intuitively.

We can compute the behavior of complex systems too — provided that we can define the mathematical relationships and formulas which represent it. In some — fairly rare — cases this is possible because we understand the mechanisms of dependence of certain variables on others and we can describe these mechanisms by means of formulas. Then the formulas or systems of equations we have set up actually represent reality — at least as long as other variables that are normally inactive do not enter suddenly into the picture. This is just the way things go with physical systems — mechanical, hydraulic, electrical — whose behavior can be considered deterministic.

Things are much more complicated when the mechanisms of dependence of certain variables on others are unknown. In these cases we can only analyze the historical series of values assumed by all the relevant variables over certain periods of time — in so far as we know them. Apart from the accuracy with which the values of the variables have been measured and recorded, in these cases the knowledge of the whole systemistic process is much less satisfactory. The equations that can be set up are empirical and, in some cases, they are expressed in table form and not by means of formal relationships. Jay W. Forrester of the Massachusetts Institute of Technology carried out in the Sixties a series of attempts to translate into formulas the dynamics of an industrial system, a whole city and, finally, the whole planet. Forrester worked out from these systems of differential equations, computer models. This approach formed the basis for the study on the Limits to Growth which constituted the first report to the Club of Rome in 1971.

Forrester's models consider two classes of variables: levels and rates. Levels are cumulative measures of certain variables. Levels which are relevant in the case of an industry are: the value of inventories, the amount of bank deposits, the sum total of accounts receivable which have to be paid by customers, the sum total of debts towards suppliers, etc.

In the case of a city, levels of interest are: the population, the number of houses of a certain type, the number of industries having certain characteristics, the number of available jobs, etc.

In the case of the planetary system, levels are: the population, total capital invested in industry and agriculture, the surface of arable land, reserves of natural resources and so on.

Rates, on the other hand, define the variations of levels over time — that is: the speed at which levels increase or decrease. In the case of an industry, relevant rates are: billings invoiced during one month (or one year), the corresponding costs of sales, collections received during a given month (or year) and so on.

In the case of a city we are interested in birth and mortality rates, immigration and emigration rates, the number of new houses built every month (or every year) and so on.

Each level is influenced by more than one rate, and each rate is in turn a function of various levels. When these dynamic models are made to operate on an electronic computer, quantums of time — or individual time steps — used are generally of one year. At each step the previous values of levels are used to compute the new values of rates and these are used to compute the variations of levels during the year.

If the initial conditions — the numerical data at the starting point — and the functional ties between the different variables were known with certainty and precision, then the computerized models built on this basis could be used for predicting the future. We must find then a way of analyzing how well we really know the laws of dependence among the various factors considered.

When we deal with socio-economic or socio-political questions, it is very rare that we are able to formulate theories, so precise to allow us the definition of mathematical formulas describing reality with the same accuracy obtained in the physical sciences. The only thing we can do, then, is to try and determine what type of regularity has been observed in the past in the occurrence of two or more factors or variables — and to suppose that the same type of relationship will be valid also in the future.

One way of checking whether our hypothesis is correct would be to accept as raw data only information concerning events that took place up to a certain time in the past. Let us suppose that we accept data concerning a certain socio-economic system, taken from the period 1900—1950. Using this data base, we can formulate a theory supposing that the variables with which we are dealing are mutually tied by formal relationships, obviously compatible with the recorded data. Then we use this theory to predict — as it were — the behavior of the system for the 30 years between 1950 and 1980. While we do this, we shall ignore for the time being the historically known events from these thirty years, which in actual fact have already elapsed. Then we compare the predictions derived from the model with the actual known events which have taken place between 1950 and 1980. If we find that predictions and actual history are quite different, we will be forced to conclude that the model lacks predictive value.

If, on the other hand, the predictions — that we would have made in 1950 based on the model — substantially coincide with history up to the present, we may conclude that the model would have made an accurate prediction 30 years ago. However, we are not authorized to suppose that the model will go on producing correct forecasts from now on. There is, 'in fact, an infinity of functions which approximate faithfully experimental data over a given interval, and that deviate from them outside the interval by very large factors.

Furthermore, we can never rule out the possibility of some future event cropping up and altering deeply the type or the very existence of the relations we had observed between the different variables. We need only think of the possible rise of armed conflict — which cannot be foreseen by means of mathematical procedures and which would change radically the socio-economic conditions of a whole region of the planet. Similar considerations can be made concerning extreme and adverse weather conditions.

We would give up all pretence of the model's predictive capability and just use it to make explicit the consequences of certain clearly defined hypotheses. One or more of the variables that define the behavior of the system can be considered as exogenous. This means that the values of these variables are chosen from the outside — arbitrarily, even if consistently with certain constraints of coherence and verisimilitude. The exogenous variables can have an effect on other variables, but they cannot be influenced by them. This device deprives the model of some of its flexibility but it may permit us to evaluate the consequences of certain strategies and it simplifies the problem considerably.

Mesarovic and Pestel, for example, have devised their global model of the world system so that it can be used in an interactive mode. This means that decision makers may insert into the model as exogenous variables some of their possible strategies. Then, later, they take note of the probable consequences to be expected within a few years and, at that point, they may decide to start all over and try again with different strategies or to steer a different course from then on. The model can be used, then, as a game for the training of decision makers.

This type of application has not been very popular as yet with statesmen. An exception is represented by the government of the Federal Republic of Germany which has financed the compilation of a version of the Mesarovic-Pestel model specialized to represent German situations. A team of economists, systems experts and planners currently use the computerized model, interpret the results and devise new interactive applications.

In other countries the quality of decisions taken (or avoided) by public decision makers justifies our doubts that they possess free will. The sequences of their actions appear, in fact, as endogenous variables, whose values are not chosen externally in order to reach a goal, but just follow each other as in the case of quasi-random natural phenomena (meteorological, etc.).

We cannot avoid considering certain variables as exogenous when the available data base is insufficient to discover regularities from which to abstract formal relationships between the variables that define the behavior of a system. In these cases we can only imagine various alternative courses of the exogenous variables, projecting them towards the future. These projections — currently called "scenarios" — are in a sense plausible stories about the future that we tell to ourselves. If we lack better data, we can only pick inconsistencies in these stories and eliminate them to obtain increased plausibility.

When we decide to create a mathematical model of the future (of an industry, a region of the world) we reveal our implicit belief in a certain determinism. On the other hand nobody can predict the future of a completely deterministic system, if the information is insufficient. When systems are extremely large, we can say that information is always insufficient, particularly if the type of event with which we want to deal has never taken place before.

Just to be concrete, suppose we want to analyze what could be the history of the world after a nuclear war, which reduces the population of the planet to 500 million people. We have never had nuclear warfare on that scale — fortunately. It has already happened, though, that the world's population has been 500 million — probably around the year 1600. This coincidence of a population figure would not be enough to make us believe that the destiny of the world after a nuclear holocaust would be similar to that which we know took place from the seventeenth century. Future history would be quite different for many reasons. The 500 million survivors would probably have a scientific knowledge much more advanced than their ancestors of four centuries ago. They would live in an environment full of destroyed cities and radioactively polluted. Above all, they would have roots and previous experiences completely different from those of the old times.

If we want to say something sensible about the subsequent history of those 500 million survivors, we cannot rely on mathematical formulas of any kind. We must try to imagine the environmental and biologic consequences of a nuclear war capable of killing 3½ billion people. We must figure where the survivors would be located on the globe and — on this basis — what would be the socio-cultural characteristics of each surviving group, which resources they would have available, and so on.

These evaluations are obviously a prerequisite to any other analysis. They would have to be carried out intuitively and — in many different alternative ways. The credibility of each of these scenarios again would have to be judged, partly based on intuition, and partly based on coherence and logical criteria. In an extreme case like this, the use of scenarios cannot be avoided — although, of course, they should be reasonably based on all the available information on location and destructive potential of nuclear weapons, target homing accuracy, reliability and reaction times of the weapons systems developed by the different countries, etc. The use of scenarios, however, can be advisable also in less extreme cases.

To produce scenarios we have to be imaginative. Brainstorming techniques have been repeatedly proposed as a powerful support to innovative and constructive imagination. Personally I think that brainstorming has brought some results in the fields of advertising and of the naming of new commercial products — but hardly in any other field.

A more promising technique appears to be brainwriting — as proposed by Geschka, Schaude and Schlicksupp in their paper "Modern Techniques for Solving Problems" (*Chemical Engineering*, August 1973). Brainwriting presupposes that the group of people who are trying to innovate together, sit around the same table — in silence. Each member of the team writes down on a sheet a couple of ideas concerning the problem or subject under discussion. Then all the sheets are collected in a sheaf at the center of the table. Each participant takes from the sheaf the notes written by someone else, reads them and adds freely other ideas which may be influenced or not by those he has just read. Brainwriting is reported to work better than brainstorming, because the more timid members of the group are not overwhelmed by the aggressive verbosity of the more extrovert. Other advantages are that many members of the group can work in parallel and that the written records can be used right away and possibly transmitted to another group to start a second stage of the same procedure. The description of the procedure is very simple: the results are apparently quite good.

There are also other modern procedures for attacking very complex problems, which can be described very simply. This does not mean that these procedures are simplistic. It may well mean that we are so ignorant in the field of complexity that we can learn something useful even from the application of unsophisticated common sense.

One obvious consideration is that each plan or program should contain no mutually contradictory aims and should be characterized by a rational structure. Yet we often note that plans, policy statements and projects presented by experts at the national and at the international level completely fail to obey these obvious requirements.

John N. Warfield has made an effort to bring some order and coherence in this sphere of activity in his book *Societal Systems — Planning, Policy and Complexity* (Wiley-Interscience, 1976). For example Warfield has subjected the document put out by the United Nations Committee for Development Planning in 1970, to a methodical critical review. This document dealt with the launching of a second decade of development and its title was *Towards Accelerated Development.* It contained no less than 55 objectives to be achieved. The loftiest (and most vague) among these were, for example, "to bring to fruition the hopes of mankind", "to comprehend the interrelations among the elements in the development process", "to diminish world tension", "to provide opportunities for a better life to all sections of the population". The more modest (and more concrete) objectives were, for example: "to improve labor force statistics", "to correct ills caused by urbanization", "to establish new towns remote from large cities".

Warfield has attempted to place all the objectives indicated in the United Nations document in a tree block diagram, in which every objective which is a prerequisite for the achievement of another more general objective, is situated at a lower level than the latter and is connected to it by a line. All the objectives turned out to be connected to at least one other objective. The document, then, appears to mirror some sort of conceptual framework. The completeness of the document appears less satisfying, if we note that:

- for less than 20% of all the goals listed there is a suggestion of a measure of achievement
- for the majority of goals, there is no indication of who should be responsible for their achievement, of what resources should be used, of which methodologies should be employed, nor of which time schedule and deadlines should be respected.

The structure of the United Nations document is then to a large extent illusory. Too many goals are not measurable, or are too vague.

It would be instructive to evaluate the credibility, feasibility and coherence of government plans and public programs in many different countries. This job is carried out in countries where criticism and political opposition are admitted — by political adversaries. However, political opponents often have no interest in objective criticism. They only try to score possibly only apparent victories in debates and controversies.

In order to render the analyses more objective and significant, Warfield has suggested more elaborate techniques based on mathematical procedures. For a detailed treatment of these techniques, it is better to refer to Warfield's book. It may be worthwhile, though, to give here at least an example of the use of binary interaction matrices.

Suppose we have chosen a number of categories of factors, which are relevant for the purposes of a project or policy measure to be implemented. These categories or classes may be, for example, objectives, resources, constraints, agencies involved,

societal sectors involved and so on. It is obviously interesting
to decide which elements of one category interact with which
elements of every other category. All the possible interactions
between elements of two categories can be described schemati-
cally by means of a matrix having a number of columns equal
to the number of elements of the first category of factors and
a number of rows equal to the number of the elements of the
other category. The matrix is binary — which means that it
is composed of elements that can have only the value 0 or the
value 1. At the intersection between a row and a column we
record the symbol 1 to denote that there is a significant interaction between the element corresponding to the column and
the element corresponding to the row. If this mutual action is
not significant, we record the symbol 0.

Let us consider first just the possible interactions between
two objectives and three possible activities or enterprises.
The two objectives are:

O_1 = increase in the number of people actively employed
O_2 = decrease in the quantity of crude oil imported per year.

The three activities are:

A_1 = industrial and commercial enterprises for the diffusion
     of solar energy
A_2 = energy conservation activities
A_3 = industrial and commercial enterprises for the produc-
     tion and diffusion of machines capable of producing
     energy through the effect of hydraulic heads produced
     by tides.

We will not argue whether the three activities are necessary
or sufficient to reach the three goals, but only whether they
interact with the two objectives. As far as activity A_3 is concerned, we suppose that the machinery under discussion can be
produced in a Mediterranean country and exported — even if
this can be true only for a part of the machines belonging to

power stations for the exploitation of tidal energy.

The interaction matrix relating objectives and activities would then be as follows:

	0_1	0_2
A_1	1	1
A_2	0	1
A_3	1	0

The value assigned to the matrix elements can be justified with easy arguments. The first activity, A_1, implies both a greater employment of manpower and a decrease in the demand for energy that has to be satisfied by recourse to imported fuel. Activity A_2 — aimed at the elimination of energy waste — would have next to no effect on the number of available jobs, but would reduce the quantity of oil imported. Finally the third activity would create new jobs, but would have no influence over the quantity of imported oil, because the power stations for exploiting tidal energy can only be exported and not installed in the same Mediterranean nation, where tides produce small heads. Let us now consider the interaction matrix between the two objectives already mentioned and certain constraints that have to be taken into account.

Let us suppose that there are 4 constraints to be considered:

C_1 = the condition that every intervention contributes to increase the gross national product of the country considered

C_2 = the condition that each intervention must not imply an availability of labor greater than the existing active population

C_3 = the condition that each intervention must not imply capital investment greater than certain ceilings

C_4 = the condition that the objectives established must not contribute to increasing inflation.

We may reasonably suppose that objective 0_1 contributes

to increase the gross national product, while objective 0_2 in all likelihood has no effect on the gross national product. We can accept the hypothesis that every intervention aimed at achieving the two objectives never comes up against a scarcity of labor — at least in the present conditions of fairly high unemployment. We can assume that the constraint concerning available capital is significant as far as the decrease in oil imports is concerned — since investments are required for finding alternative sources of energy. We may think instead that any increase in employment would come about through the exploitation of unused industrial capacity, without new investment. Finally, we may suppose that the two objectives might have some effect on inflationary processes — hopefully a positive effect.

Under these hypotheses the interaction matrix between objectives and constraints is as follows:

	C_1	C_2	C_3	C_4
0_1	1	0	0	1
0_2	0	0	1	1

We must now build a matrix of interactions between activities and constraints, having four columns and three rows. We could build it, reasoning out the mutual influences between constraints and activities, as we did in the two previous cases. But we could not rule out the possibility that in this third case we would follow a line of reasoning not logically congruent with those followed in the former cases.

An alternative solution is to make explicit the logical implications already used in the construction of the first two matrixes. This can be done by computing the constraints—activities interaction matrix as their Boolean product.

The w elements of the products matrix are obtained from the y elements of the activities—objectives matrix and from the z elements of the objectives—constraints matrix by means of the following relationships, in which the products are Boolean (carried out according to the rules: $0.0=0$; $0.1=0$; $1.0=0$; $1.1=1$) and the sums are Boolean (carried out according to the rules: $0+0=0$; $0+1=1+0=1+1=1$). As can easily be seen, this Boolean product between matrixes merely expresses the transitivity property. The first formula below means that, if A_1 and C_1 both interact with 0_1 (or 0_2), then they also interact with each other.

$$w_{11} = y_{11}\, z_{11} + y_{12}\, z_{21}$$
$$w_{12} = y_{11}\, z_{12} + y_{12}\, z_{22}$$
$$w_{13} = y_{11}\, z_{13} + y_{12}\, z_{23}$$
$$w_{14} = y_{11}\, z_{14} + y_{12}\, z_{24}$$

$$w_{21} = y_{21}\, z_{11} + y_{22}\, z_{21}$$
$$w_{22} = y_{21}\, z_{12} + y_{22}\, z_{22}$$
$$w_{23} = y_{21}\, z_{13} + y_{22}\, z_{23}$$
$$w_{24} = y_{21}\, z_{14} + y_{22}\, z_{24}$$

$$w_{31} = y_{31}\, z_{11} + y_{32}\, z_{21}$$
$$w_{32} = y_{31}\, z_{12} + y_{32}\, z_{22}$$
$$w_{33} = y_{31}\, z_{13} + y_{32}\, z_{23}$$
$$w_{34} = y_{31}\, z_{14} + y_{32}\, z_{24}$$

For greater clarity the elements of the three matrixes are repeated with their symbols in tabular form as follows:

	0_1	0_2		C_1	C_2	C_3	C_4
A_1	y_{11}	y_{12}		w_{11}	w_{12}	w_{13}	w_{14}
A_2	y_{21}	y_{22}		w_{21}	w_{22}	w_{23}	w_{24}
A_3	y_{31}	y_{32}		w_{31}	w_{32}	w_{33}	w_{34}
			0_1	z_{11}	z_{12}	z_{13}	z_{14}
			0_2	z_{21}	z_{22}	z_{23}	z_{24}

Consequently the interaction matrix between activities and constraints looks like this:

	C_1	C_2	C_3	C_4
A_1	1	0	1	1
A_2	0	0	1	1
A_3	1	0	0	1

We can interpret this last matrix by stating, for example, that the only one of the three activities foreseen that does not exert any influence over the gross national product is energy conservation. We can also deduce from the matrix the consequence — at first sight surprising — that the launching of activities aimed at producing tide-powered energy plants for exportation should never come up against constraints limiting the amount of available capital. It is quite possible that there should be disagreement about this latter statement. If so, we should go and search for its genesis in the hypotheses made concerning objectives and their interactions with activities and constraints. These hypotheses can then be revised, and the matrixes changed accordingly. The importance of the procedure described lies in its guarantee of compatibility between the three matrices produced.

The example given here may seem trivial. The procedure, though, is not trivial when the categories of factors considered are numerous and in each there are a few dozen factors. The procedure is also important because it helps to deal with heterogeneous elements — social, physical, technical, economic — in one single structure. The input data used can be supplied also by people, who would be unable to understand the mathematical aspects of the procedure. The procedure permits us to decompose the systems we are analyzing into congruent and smaller subsets, so we can have a better grasp of the problems and of their solutions.

R. F. Erlandson of the Bell Laboratories has defined in 1975, a set of variables which can be used to define the phenomena of interaction between systems, between subsystems, between control parameters and policy measures.

I hope I have succeeded in proving that interdisciplinary efforts are a necessity — not just a fashion — if we want to solve complex socio-economic and socio-technological problems. We must also recognize that it is not enough for an endeavor to be inter-disciplinary — it should also be meaningful and rational.

These concepts are not even understood by contemporary

proponents of solutions which are just called innovative, but refuse reason and rationality. Often these false innovations are presented by uncivilized, cruel and violent individuals who use the weapons of terrorism and coercion — although they claim that over the long term these weapons will be abandoned and utopia will be reached.

Social, economic and technological progress cannot do without traditional rationality. On the contrary we should renew it learning to master more subtle and complex procedures — apt to cope with the growing complexity of society, of economy and of technology. All this is true whatever field we are active in.

We can conclude that modest technologies will be usable to simplify many problems, to minimize many investments and to create new jobs — but most decisions concerning innovative enterprises for establishing modest technologies will be highly complex. Any faith in the contrary would be illusory.

Bibliography

Bastiat, M. F., *Sophismes Economiques*, Bruxelles, 1851.

Bossel, H. (ed.), *Concepts and Tools of Computer Assisted Policy Analysis*, Birkhäuser, 1977.

Burdick, E. and Lederer, B., *The Ugly American*, Fawcett Publ., 1958.

Casatello, F., *Robinson '80*, Mondadori, 1979.

Congdon, R. J. (ed.), *Lectures on Socially Appropriate Technologies*, Technische Hogeschool Eindhoven, 1975.

de Solla Price, D. J., *Little Science, Big Science*, Columbia University Press, 1963.

Erlandson, R. F., *Systems Interaction Mechanisms*, I.E.E.E. Transactions on Systems, Man and Cybernetics, January 1975, p. 116–23.

Forrester, J. W., *Industrial Dynamics*, The MIT Press, 1961.

Forrester J. W., *Urban Dynamics*, The MIT Press, 1969.

Forrester, J. W., *World Dynamics*, Wright-Allen, 1971.

Friedman, M., Foreign Economic Aid — Means and Objectives, *The Yale Review*, Summer 1958.

Galbraith, J. K., *The New Industrial State*, Houghton-Mifflin, 1967.

Gurr, T., *Why Men Rebel*, Princeton University Press, 1972.

Jéquier, N. (ed.), *Appropriate Technologies; Problems and Promises*, Development Centre OECD, 1976.

Keynes, J. M., *Essays in Persuasion*, The Norton Library, 1963.

Lipsey, R. G. and Lancaster, K. K., The General Theory of Second Best, *Review of Economic Studies*, Vol. XXIVn, 1956–57, pp. 11–32.

Mensch, G., *Das technologische Patt*, Umschau Verlag, 1975.

Mishan, E. J., *Cost/Benefit Analysis*, Unwin University Books, 1972.

Pincus, A., *Reshaping the World Economy*, Prentice-Hall, 1968.

Samuelson, P., *Economics*, McGraw-Hill, 1964.

Schumacher, E. F., *Small is Beautiful*, Abacus, 1975.

Taube, M., *Computers and Common Sense*, McGraw-Hill, 1961.

Tinbergen, J. (ed.), *RIO, Reshaping the International Order*, Dutton, 1976.

Tucker, R. W., *The Inequality of Nations*, Basic Books, 1977.

Vacca, R., *The Coming Dark Age*, Anchor-Doubleday, 1974.
Warfield, J. N., *Societal Systems*, Wiley-Interscience, 1976.
Zartman, I. W., *The 50% Solution*, Anchor-Doubleday, 1976.

Name Index

167

Subject Index

in industrialized countries 88 ff
organizations active in promoting (list) 134
preliminary studies for 79
protection of 90
risks run by ventures 116 ff
strategies for introducing 132 ff
see also Alternative t.; Intermediate t.

Nation state concept, outdated 20
Negotiations, trend towards 16
Neutrality of science and technology 38 ff
Nuclear holocaust scenario 155
Nuclear power produced using fissile materials from disassembled nuclear weapons 121

Pareto optimality 96, 99
Participation 149
Photovoltaic cells 66 ff
Pollution risks 115
Predictive value of dynamic models 153 ff
Price and cost structures, their arbitrariness xiii, 101, 109
Productivity, increase of in U.S. 48
Productivity reduced to 1/6 (Schumacher's proposal criticized) 35
Protectionism 62 ff
Pumps driven by bicycles 1

Quality control 126
Quality of life 31
Quantification of arguments 36

Random factors affecting success of innovation 131
Rational expectations (theory of) 50 ff
Recycling materials 90
Red Sea, project of closing with dam 63
Relative deprivation 15
Research and Development investments 53 ff
Revolutionary processes 42
RIO Report 13 ff
Risk of doing business 112 ff
Risk perception, faulty 117 ff
Risks 113 ff

Safety in industry 115 ff
Scenarios of the future 155
Science, definition of 38
Scientific development growth, slowdown of 19 ff
Second best xxx
Shadow prices 109 ff
Simplification of production tasks vs. efforts in training personnel 80
Small Is Beautiful, E. F. Schumacher 24 ff
Solar energy 63 ff
Structural multi-use elements 85
Sub-pessimization 100
Superpowers, as custodians of world order 22 ff
Supply and demand mechanism 97 ff
Switzerland, economy of 49
Systems Dynamics National Model (J. W. Forrester) 56
Systems engineering
ignored by Schumacher 25
procedures 43, 149